The Joy of Ministry

The Joy of Ministry

Thomas W. Currie III

Westminster John Knox Press
LOUISVILLE • LONDON

Scripture quotations from the New Revised Standard Version of the Bible are copyright © 1989 by the Division of Christian Education of the National Council of the Churches of Christ in the U.S.A. and are used by permission.

Quotations from Karl Barth's *Church Dogmatics*, ed. G. W. Bromiley and T. F. Torrance (Edinburgh: T. & T. Clark, 1969), are reprinted with permission of the publisher, The Continuum International Publishing Group.

Quotations from *Open Secrets* by Richard Lischer, copyright © 2001 by Richard Lischer. Used by permission of Doubleday, a division of Random House, Inc.

Quotations from "Minimum Salary," a commencement address given by Thomas W. Currie at Union Theological Seminary and Presbyterian School of Christian Education, and published in *The Presbyterian Outlook*, July 11–18, are reprinted with permission of the Presbyterian Outlook Foundation Inc.

Quotations from David Johnson's "Making Theology Come Alive in the Parish," *Pro Ecclesia* 3, no. 4 (1994): 401–2, are reprinted with permission of Rowman & Littlefield Publishers, Inc.

Book design by Sharon Adams
Cover design by Mark Abrams
Cover art: Uva moscadella nera [Moscadella black grapes] by Giorgio Gallesio from the book Pomona Italiana: Trattato degli alberi fruttiferi conteneate la Descrizione delle megliori varietáa dei Frutte coltivati in Italia (published 1817–39). Courtesy of the NYPL Digital Library.

First edition
Published by Westminster John Knox Press
Louisville, Kentucky

This book is printed on acid-free paper that meets the American National Standards Institute Z39.48 standard. ∞

PRINTED IN THE UNITED STATES OF AMERICA

08 09 10 11 12 13 14 15 16 17— 10 9 8 7 6 5 4 3 2 1

Library of Congress Cataloging-in-Publication Data

Currie, Thomas W.
    The joy of ministry / Thomas W. Currie III. — 1st ed.
    p. cm.
    ISBN 978-0-664-23109-5 (alk. paper)
    1. Pastoral theology. 2. Joy—Religious aspects—Christianity. I. Title.
    BV4011.3.C87   2008
    253—dc22
                             2007034277

For Chris and Stephanie and Thomas,
and for Kate and Chad,
and for Anne,
who have brought me great joy

Contents

Acknowledgments

Around 1980, I attended a continuing education event at Austin Presbyterian Theological Seminary. The featured speaker that week was my revered teacher from New College days, Professor Thomas F. Torrance. I came to that conference feeling weary and much oppressed with my duties as a pastor of a small church in central Texas, and I was hoping to talk some theology with an old friend and valued mentor. And indeed, that was one of the gifts I received that week. But something else happened as well.

One of the other participants in the course was John Rogers, who was then pastor of First Presbyterian Church, Shreveport, Louisiana. I did not know John at the time, but we soon became good friends, both of us convinced of the importance of theology and preaching for the life of the church. As we left to go to supper one night, John turned to me and said, "Isn't ministry wonderful?"

His question caught me off guard. "How naive could he be?" I thought. Yet I soon realized his question was not the chirpiness of an inexperienced and innocent pastor, but a question asked from the very depths of the faith. His question put me on the spot. What would I say about ministry? Something smart-alecky to indicate that I knew how unwonderful it often feels? Something skeptical that would qualify "wonderful," reducing it to something unmiraculous, bland, and flat, just another job? Or something coldly indifferent, a silence that simply looked the other way. In the event, what I mumbled was simply, "Yes. . . . Yes, it is." As rueful as that reply might have seemed and as timidly voiced as it was, I will always be grateful to John Rogers for forcing me to think about ministry not in terms of my own weariness or "failure" or "success" but in terms of the gift and the task of pointing to Jesus Christ. The ministry of this Lord is literally filled with wonder, which is not to say that it is filled with exhilaration and euphoria, but that its sheer existence is an ongoing miracle whose grace is both relentlessly embarrassing and surprisingly joyful. If one cannot acknowledge that from the beginning, then the work of ministry will always seem a dutiful chore at best, a sad and gloomy affair at worst.

So I want to acknowledge, first of all, my debt to my friend John Rogers, who many years later became my pastor at Covenant Presbyterian Church in Charlotte, North Carolina. John has read this manuscript and has been generous with his suggestions and comments.

I also want to thank Edward Newberry, who pastors Memorial Presbyterian Church in Charlotte and was gracious enough to read this manuscript and to offer detailed notes, suggestions, and comments. Few pastors exemplify the Reformed way of being Christian better than Edward Newberry, and I am glad to acknowledge my ongoing debt to him.

In addition, I must add a word of thanks to William Willimon, now bishop of the North Alabama Conference of the United Methodist Church. Like so many who have attempted to pastor during the last several years, I have received a great deal from reading Will Willimon's many books and articles. His passion for an ecclesial and theological understanding of the role of the pastor has deeply informed my own efforts to speak of the joy of ministry. I am grateful for Bishop Willimon's reading of my manuscript and for his suggestions and encouragement.

In 2001, I was called to serve as dean of Union-PSCE at Charlotte, a new extension seminary of Union Theological Seminary and Presbyterian School of Christian Education in Richmond, Virginia. This new venture has given me an opportunity to help shape a future generation of pastors and teachers, an opportunity that would not have come to me without the unflagging support of the president of Union-PSCE at that time, Louis Weeks. I wish to record my sincere gratitude to him for his patience, wisdom, and encouragement along this path. He has been a wonderful mentor and a good companion.

Ministry is not inimical to friendships. Since assuming my present duties, I have been blessed to count Bill White as my friend. Bill and his wife, Betsy, have served as elders in Myers Park Presbyterian Church in Charlotte, North Carolina, where he has taught the senior high Sunday class for the past fifty-two years. A successful real estate developer, Bill chaired the board of Union Theological Seminary for many years and has been the driving force behind the establishment of a theological seminary in Charlotte. Bill has been a good friend, lifting me up when I have been low and puncturing my more inflated moments with his dry wit and reality-inducing barbs.

My son, Chris Currie, is pastor of the Presbyterian congregation in Calypso, North Carolina. I am deeply grateful to him for his reading of this manuscript and his willingness to offer correction both theological and grammatical in nature. The two fields are more closely related, he reminds me, than one might think. I am glad to note that the work of the ministry has diminished neither his sense of humor nor the joy to be found in setting his father straight.

I also would like to thank my sister, Alison Meier, and her husband, Dieter, for their willingness to read and offer suggestions for some of my translations in this book from the German.

The place where I have worked for the past several years is filled with gifted teachers and valued colleagues. I thank Richard Boyce, Pamela Mitchell-Legg, Rodney Sadler, and Sue Setzer for their friendship, encouragement, and commitment to the ministry of preaching and teaching. It is a gift to serve with such talented teachers and scholars. I also want to thank my colleague Terry Johns for her help in this project, particularly her ability to help me find quiet time to write and her zealous protection of that. She also has helped me navigate the options available on my own computer, which otherwise would have overwhelmed me. In addition, I would like to acknowledge Susan Griner, Susan Hickok, David Mayo, Jan Parler, and Nadine Ellsworth-Moran, colleagues at Union-PSCE at Charlotte who have encouraged me along the way.

For the past few years it has been my privilege to be part of a group of pastor-theologians whose work has been sponsored by the Center of Theological Inquiry in Princeton. The leader of this effort and the former head of CTI is Wallace Alston, whose understanding of and commitment to the theological basis of ministry has been a gift to countless ministers at work in the church today and has inspired my reflections in this book. Wallace has read part of this manuscript. I am indebted to him for his comments and encouragement, even when I have chosen at times to go in a different direction. I am also indebted to Jim Haddix, another member of this pastor-theologian group, who graciously took the time to read my entire manuscript and to offer his insights, encouragement, and corrections.

I also thank Donald McKim and Dan Braden of Westminster John Knox Press. Their wisdom and guidance have made this book better than it otherwise would have been. I am grateful for the encouragement of Sheldon Sorge, formerly associate for theology and worship for the Presbyterian Church (U.S.A.) and now the associate director of the Louisville Institute. Sheldon's work for the past several years has been to lift up for the church the importance of forming ministers whose identity is shaped by their theological vocation. I hope this book will be of help in that crucial endeavor.

For twenty-five years, I served as a pastor. The first twelve and a half years, I served Brenham Presbyterian Church in Brenham, Texas. In 1989, we moved to Kerrville, Texas, where I served First Presbyterian Church until June 2001. One of the dangers in looking back on one's ministry is the temptation to romanticize those days and depict them as one triumph or joy after another. My memory is indeed filled with many occasions of joy, but I also remember how hard things were at times, how discouraged and tired I became, how exhausting ministry often was. And yet, and yet, those days *were* wonderful, not obviously so and rarely spectacularly so, but filled with the ordinary grace of life. I want to acknowledge the gifts of those two congregations to me, not least of which was to teach me about that "cluster of grapes" that makes ministry a joy.

This book is dedicated to my children and their families: to Chris and his wife, Stephanie, and their son, Thomas; to my daughter Kate and her husband, Chad; and to my daughter Anne. They and my wife, Peggy, have shared in this ministry with me. Perhaps they have shared more than they would have liked, but I want to acknowledge all of them with deepest gratitude.

Chapter One

A Cluster of Grapes

Joy and the Task of Ministry

Q.1. What is your only comfort in life and in death?
A. That I belong—body and soul, in life and in death—not
to myself but to my faithful Savior, Jesus Christ.
> —Heidelberg Catechism

Consider the lilies of the field, how they grow; they toil not,
neither do they spin.
> —Matthew 6:28 (KJV)

This is not a how-to book on ministry. Nor is it a book that seeks to improve one's mood or offer inspirational nuggets of pastoral insight. Rather, this book seeks to reflect on the beauty of the church's theological task and the joy of the church's ministry.

Neither this beauty nor this joy is self-evident. Indeed, nothing is easier for mainline Protestant pastors to do these days than to despair over the life of the church. One thoughtful critique of ecumenical Protestantism concludes its analysis by invoking Psalm 102:14 and inviting those who still care about the church to love her very rubble and pity the dust that remains of her life.[1] Such dust is not hard to find. It is often on display in the long and very serious meetings of the church's governing bodies, meetings that are able to suck the delight and joy of ministry into a darkness from which no light easily emerges. The church's theological task, at least as practiced within much of the academy, is equally capable

1

of plunging one into a rubble-strewn despair—what the monks, following the psalmist, called "the destruction that wastes at noonday"—so much so that joy seems the last gift one might associate with this vital task of the church.

This is the way Christian discipleship often feels. Following Jesus Christ never has been a series of mountaintop experiences regularly yielding ecstatic moments of unalloyed happiness. The gifts of the Spirit are rarely quantifiable and never self-evident. Rather, the pattern of Christian discipleship has always been deeply incarnational, which is to say that the joy of the faith has always been hidden amid the quite unglamorous work that love undertakes in the name of Jesus Christ, including careful study, listening, waiting, asking, cultivating, and preparing. Eugene Peterson has compared the work of ministry to the drudgery of farmwork, "similar to cleaning out the barn, mucking out the stalls, spreading manure, pulling weeds," all of which he notes is a far cry from riding a black stallion in a parade to the acclaim of all.[2] He is right to caution us against a lust for the spiritually glamorous. However, the regular work of a pastor is not just difficult or even labor intensive but also distressingly full of the pain that comes with seeking to lead a community of reconciliation, attempting the impossible work of loving those with whom we disagree, reaching out to those whose lives have been disrupted or even broken, seeking to speak a word of grace to an angry and hurting collection of sinners.

Yet all of this accounts for only part of the challenge that faces most ministers today, and indeed, all of this could be cheerfully borne if something else were not amiss. And what is that? There may be a number of ways of getting at what is wrong but perhaps it would be most helpful simply to say that there seems to be a lack of wonder or sense of mystery or wellspring of joy that accompanies and sustains Christian ministry today. Conceived as a task, the ministry is easily described and even evaluated in terms of professional leadership skills. Conceived as an organization, the church can easily be described and evaluated in terms of its "product" and its success in the marketplace. Conceived as a set of ideas, the gospel can easily be reduced to critical theory and explanation. But undertaken with such models in mind, the church's life and ministry inevitably become something we achieve and even manage, losing the lightness (and the mystery) of their being gifts of grace and acquiring instead the heaviness of self that eventually crushes those who are condemned either to succeed or to fail. Orthodox theologian David B. Hart probes more deeply when he suggests that what ails us is a kind of "metaphysical boredom," the residue of an Enlightenment liberalism that has ceased to hope or wonder or imagine. All it can offer the church is the power of its critique; it is unable to be creative or even procreative.[3] In any case, the joy of the Christian life has leached out of our life together and the very heaviness of our constructive efforts, however earnestly undertaken, now prevents us from embracing, even ruefully, the great comedy of redemption.

One might object that a lack of joy is hardly the most damning thing to be put against the church's account today. The church's failure to live out its own great ends is so manifest and so discouraging that a perceived lack of joy in its life and witness seems at best a petty complaint. After all, if one wants joy, television provides happy and smiling evangelists only too eager to have us partake of their positive attitude, especially if we do not ask too many hard questions about hunger or defeat or death. Joy, as a therapeutic commodity, has been sold (and bought) so often that one might well ask if authentic discipleship might not be better off without it.

And, more to the point, what about those hard questions, particularly the questions of hunger and defeat and death? What kind of joy is it that might encompass such things? We do well, one might think, to engage such principalities and powers at all, much less to do so joyfully. What, to paraphrase a popular song from not so long ago, does joy have to do with it?

This book proposes that nothing is more crucial to the future of the church's own life and ministry than the recovery of the gospel's gift of joy. This joy, Jesus tells us, is the rightful property of his disciples, something that no one will be able to take from them: "I will see you again, and your hearts will rejoice, and no one will take your joy from you" (John 16:22). Such a gift, far from being a positive attitude or constantly upbeat mood, is best described as a deep confidence, even a kind of astonished laughter because of the discovery that there is One at work in our world more central to our stories than we are to ourselves. Such joy is always a surprise. "When the LORD restored the fortunes of Zion, we were like those who dream. Then our mouth was filled with laughter, and our tongue with shouts of joy" (Ps. 126:1). Similarly, the disciples on the road to Emmaus, having had to explain the reality of things to the dullard who had fallen into step with them along the road, discover in his presence One who singed their hearts and revealed a quite unsuspected reality which they (and the eleven) could not quite take in for the joy of it all (Luke 24:41). Such joy, while not a mood, is a gift that issues in a certain boldness of spirit, a kind of unapologetic delight in the beauty and truth of Easter, which soon takes the form of "proclaiming the kingdom of God and teaching about the Lord Jesus Christ with all boldness [*parrhesias*, boldly, joyfully] and unhindered" (Acts 28:31).

One person who has reflected a good deal on the theological significance of joy is Father Alexander Schmemann, the late dean of St. Vladimir's Seminary in New York. His *Journals*, published in 2000, have more than one entry on this topic. There he writes, "I think God will forgive everything except lack of joy; when we forget that God created the world and saved it. Joy is not one of the components of Christianity, it's the *tonality* of Christianity that penetrates *everything*—faith and vision. Where there is no joy, Christianity becomes fear and therefore torture."[4]

What Schmemann notices above all is how joy has been excluded by the way the modern world (and the postmodern even more so) conceives of itself and tells its own story. The modern world, Schmemann thinks, is suspicious of joy and has much more confidence in such concepts as the pursuit of happiness, whose serious work will never be confused with an irresponsible celebration of grace.

> How can one be joyful, when so many people suffer? When so many things are to be done? How can one indulge in festivals and celebrations when people expect from us "serious"

answers to their problems? Consciously or unconsciously Christians have accepted the whole ethos of our joyless and business-minded culture. They believe that the only way to be taken "seriously" by the "serious"—that is, by a modern man—is to be serious, and, therefore, to reduce to a symbolic "minimum" what in the past was so tremendously central in the life of the church—the joy of a feast.[5]

Schmemann is onto something. The misery of mainline Protestantism today is not best described by rounding up the usual suspects of declining numbers of members, a smaller place in the religious marketplace and correspondingly less influence in the culture, an aging membership bitterly divided over unwinnable arguments concerning human sexuality or some other political or cultural issue. Rather, what describes the true pathos of our situation is a certain joylessness, an inability to "lift up our hearts" in response to the risen Lord, who invites us to participate in his victory over sin and death. Here we seem to be strangely inarticulate, like the guest invited to the marriage feast who comes without a wedding garment and just stands there speechless. We do not know what to do. So instead we become busy. We do good. We do generous (and very necessary) things, from feeding the hungry to building houses, hospitals, and schools. We plan well. We are an extraordinarily helpful and compassionate people. But all of this too often indicates not the overflowing of joy in our lives so much as the determined flight from such a gift. For such a gift threatens to reveal our own neediness, our fear of losing control to some "irresponsible" grace. The pursuit of happiness would never embarrass us in this way. Indeed, it regularly confirms us in our own self-sufficiency, which is why we prefer it to the gift of joy.

All of this leaves us with a disquieting sense that something at the heart of our life together as a church is missing or has gone disastrously wrong. We have grown busy but not joyful. We can plan for rejoicing "events" and study the matter at length; we can even frame worship services in the name of joy; but the joy of the gospel that Jesus insists is rightfully ours (John 16:22) remains, for us, frustratingly elusive and oddly inarticulate.

There is a danger here, a big one, that "joy" may be equated with "fun" or even "uplift." That is how the pursuit of happiness tends to understand the gift of joy. In his book on the sacraments, Schmemann notes:

> The modern world has relegated joy to the category of "fun" and "relaxation." It is justified and permissible on our "time off"; it is a concession and compromise [to the serious business of life]. And Christians have come to believe this, or rather they have ceased to believe that [joy has] something to do precisely with the "serious problems" of life itself, may even be *the* Christian answer to them.[6]

But fun is not what joy is about. Indeed, the real enemy of joy is that self-absorption that seeks to be endlessly entertained, constantly distracted, always busy. The pursuit of happiness is a hard taskmaster and like most tyrants is suspicious of anything resembling Sabbath rest, much preferring the 24/7 economy of convenience, a consumer culture that is on all the time. In fact, the disappearance of Sabbath in our culture and the corresponding passion for "amusing ourselves to death"[7] should offer us a clue as to why joy is so difficult for us today and why our desperate activity has such a nihilistic edge to it.

Part of the Orthodox liturgy reads, "For through the Cross, joy came into the whole world."[8] Such a statement will strike many as weird or nonsensical. That God redeems the world from misery, from boredom, and even from its own desperate efforts to distract itself from itself, through the cross, and does so in such a way that joy enters our world, seems counterintuitive if not paradoxical. The cross can be viewed as tragic, even a tragic necessity, which makes of Jesus a heroic example of noble self-sacrifice. That we can believe. Or perhaps, with Mel Gibson, we find that the cross can make some sort of sense if it authenticates our status as worthy of redemption, especially by emphasizing the gruesome violence of Jesus' own noble suffering. Yet what if the cross is the way joy enters our world? What if precisely at the point where Christ declares his work to be finished, it is finished also with our grim efforts to justify ourselves? Hebrews 12:2 insists that Christ endured the cross "for the sake of the joy that was set before him." Might salvation be deliverance from the very joylessness that our self-absorbed lust for salvation demands? Might the gift of joy be the mark of true freedom even as it is the sign of genuine humility, the true evidence of self-forgetfulness? If salvation means forgetting self, why would joy not be at the heart of the church's proclamation? After all, is this not why such joy is a miracle and not a pursuit? And is this not why Scripture so often portrays salvation as a party, a feast, a banquet, where we are invited "to sit and eat"?[9]

"For through the Cross, joy came into the whole world." This is the strange economy of grace, the odd way the divine comedy narrates the gift of the gospel, the way we are drawn into the dance of God's triune life. That life is no stranger to the events of Good Friday or even to the terrible silence of Holy Saturday. Rather, it encompasses such dereliction and death within its own depths and, quite without our aid, is able to move the stone away from the dead-certain "realities" of which we are so sure. There the beauty and glory of a day beyond what we could imagine or conceive is revealed. Here is the joy that the cross has so strangely inserted into our world: the joy of God; the joy of Father, Son, and Holy Spirit, whose triune life traces the terms of God's making time and space for us to rejoice in him. Such joy has ever baffled those who have received it. Even the disciples hardly knew what to make of it. The resurrection narratives are full of such wonderful stumbles, from Mary Magdalene's mistaking Jesus for the gardener, to the discouraged disciples on their way to Emmaus (a town synonymous with the sad wisdom of resignation and loss), to the stories of Peter and Thomas and the embarrassing grace that delivers them into joy. As Luke says of them all, "While in their joy they were disbelieving . . ." (Luke 24:41).

❧❧❧❧❧❧❧❧

If joy is central to the church's life and ministry, how do we stumble upon it? How is such a gift recovered?

In one sense the answer to this question seems pitifully inadequate. It takes a miracle. The gospel never gives us a three-step strategy for joy, any more than it gives us a formula for living faith-fully. It is possible, Jesus tells us, to keep all ten of the command-ments and still miss the only thing that matters. If the answer were a formula, then the law of Moses would have been enough to redeem Israel and indeed, the whole world. But in truth, neither Israel nor the church could keep the law, and, worse, the tempta-tion to believe that they could made of the law an idol by which both Israel and the church sought to avoid God's grace, celebrat-ing themselves and their own virtues. That is why Paul insists that "all have sinned and fall short of the glory of God" (Rom. 3:23) and why he insists that salvation comes not through the keeping of torah but through the grace of our Lord Jesus Christ.

Reducing the scandal of grace to a formula is a typical response of modernity to faith. Having mastered the formula, we can then dismiss the person who gave us the formula. That, Søren Kierkegaard reminds us, is the difference between Socratic knowledge, in which the teacher seeks to render himself super-fluous, and the knowledge of faith, in which one never ceases to be dependent on the Teacher.[10]

In answer to the question of "How?" the church has always said that it requires a miracle of the Holy Spirit. And however unsat-isfying that answer might seem to some, it does have the virtue of reminding us that Christian discipleship is not an achievement but something God does within us, a gift of the Holy Spirit. Here too, or perhaps here especially, we are, as Luther knew, beggars, but beggars who need not be ashamed of their begging.

"All begins with a miracle," Schmemann insists, not with an explanation or argument or proof.

> I feel tired of the noise and petty intrigues that surround the Church, of the absence of breathing space, of silence, of rhythm, of all that is present in the Gospel. Maybe that is why I love an empty church, where the *Church* speaks through *silence*. I love everything that usually seems to be "in between" (to walk on a sunny morning to work, to look at a sunset, to quietly sit a while), that which may not be impor-

tant, but which alone, it seems to me, is that chink through which a mysterious ray of light shines.[11]

One "waits for God," which means, as Simone Weil might say, not that one hangs around waiting for God to do something but that one "pays attention," another name for worship.[12] Perhaps one begins to notice other beggars, some of them in great need of food or medicine or housing, and in seeking to share something of life's goods with them discovers the presence of God already in their midst. Or perhaps one is simply surprised or disturbed by joy's unlikely presence and is left to wonder what to do with one's gratitude in the face of such a miracle.[13] According to one account, this was the answer the American writer John Cheever gave for going to worship. "I go for the Eucharist. If I didn't, I wouldn't know what to do with my gratitude."[14]

What is one to do with one's gratitude? Such a question does not always make sense in a world that believes so strongly in its own achieving. Worship, for instance, seems so unproductive, even useless. To make sense of it, we think it must become assimilated to something more useful: entertainment, a good cause, a quantifiable definition of success, even critical thinking. Yet the self-centeredness that funds such views threatens not so much to take away the believer's joy—that it cannot do—but to blind us to its presence. Again, Father Schmemann has some thoughts concerning the lengths to which we will go to avoid the embarrassment of our own gratitude. Once he was invited to speak at two elite college campuses in New England. On his way back to New York, he wrote these thoughts:

> While looking yesterday at all these eyes fixed upon me during the lecture, I thought (and thought again while driving home) about what is education, upbringing. What fills the life of these huge luxurious colleges, exuding such well-being, nobility, power, surrounded by parks, reflected in the water of its pools? "We teach to think, we teach to question . . ." analysis, criticism, reflection. But talking to some

students, I realized that before criticism, maybe even before any facts of knowledge consciously or subconsciously, they expect something else. Inspiration? Truth? Meaning of life? Those are clichés, but they are it—denied with fear and contempt by contemporary academic psychology and ideology. They deny any inspiration, any vision. These youths rush with total delight to any imitation of religion, radicalism, transcendental meditation, communes. Nothing, nobody educates, directs them, nurtures them. That which created these colleges, which they still externally reflect, has been thrown away—i.e., an image, a vision. Education used to be based on a vision, concentrated on service. Life was important, beautiful, and the light of life as service was nurturing. Poor are the youth who are offered only "critical approaches."[15]

In contrast, he speaks of the joy to be found in the ordinary life of a local congregation. "I love parish feasts, community celebrations. During the liturgy, I thought: What in my life gives me pure joy? Slanting rays of sun in church during a service."[16] An ordinary gift, yet just so, everything.

In another place he writes of walking in a blighted section of an old suburb of Paris late one winter afternoon and seeing an old couple sitting on a park bench together. "They were sitting hand in hand, in silence, enjoying the pale light, the last warmth of the season. In silence: all words had been said, all passion exhausted, all storms at peace—yet all of it was now *present*, in this silence, in this light, in this warmth, in this silent unity of hands. Present— and ready for eternity, ripe for joy."[17] The joy described here is not depicted in terms of a sexually vigorous couple lolling on the beach in the sun, but a couple who seem to be participating in the gift that life has been and is, who have shared that gift with each other, and who receive it each day from the hand of God. Here is a joy that is not seeking to be helpful or smart or successful but is recognized in that phrase from sacramental theology, that is, in its "real presence," a gift that has left the spectacular, exotic, ecstatic behind only to be present amid the ordinary gifts of life. Here Christ's presence discovers us. Yet just so, here is also a great mystery, not a commodity that can be consumed or rendered useful but a gift of One who simply delights and makes the heart joyful. Others have noticed this gift as well.

One of the most remarkable novels of the past several years is David James Duncan's *The Brothers K*. In this story, which is as full of heartrending joy as it is rich in insight about ministry, there is a character named Everett Chance, the oldest son in a large family of Seventh-day Adventists. Everett is smart, clever, self-centered, and funny. He soon rejects both the faith and the church of his overbearing mother and, having escaped to the more open-minded university campus, makes a name for himself as an opponent of the war in Vietnam and a journalist of biting wit. Though his amorous conquests in college are many, the one girl he loves, Natasha, remains disconcertingly resistant to his charms. After Everett burns his draft card and flees to Canada, he finds that no one there is much interested in his wit or his convictions, and he struggles to make a life.

Out of the blue, Natasha comes for a visit, and for forty-five days Everett knows more joy than he thought possible in this life. And then, just as unaccountably, she leaves, and Everett falls into a deep depression and almost loses himself entirely. One day in spring, he finds himself walking in a meadow of buttercups when their utter beauty overwhelms him. In a letter to Natasha, he writes of falling to his knees and "vanishing" in this sea of buttercups, as if suddenly he had fallen into what he calls "a Gratitude Zone" that was as full of joy at the coming of spring as he was to find himself suddenly grateful for life. Later, trying to sort out what to do with this gratitude, he writes Natasha of this "you" which alone had kept him from doing himself in.

> Not you, Tash. I mean this other you. I refuse to resort to Uppercase here. But you hear me. And I feel you. I mean you, the who or whatever you are, being or non-being, that somehow comes to us and somehow consoles us. I don't know your name. I don't understand you. I don't know how to address you. I don't like people who think they do. But it's you alone, I begin to feel, who sends me this woman's love . . .

and this new hope and stupid gratitude. . . . So: O thing that
consoles. How clumsily I thank you.[18]

Everett eventually is called to preach a sermon to his home
church (begging the congregation for help for his injured brother,
Irwin), becoming, for a moment, what he formerly despised, a
preacher of the Word. That is where his gratitude has led him.

Though Duncan's story is not an updated version of *The Brothers Karamazov*, Dostoyevsky's novel also has a great deal to say
about the nature of ministry. One of the brothers is Alyosha, a
young man studying for the priesthood. At the end of the novel,
Alyosha preaches to the boys who have come to be his disciples:

> You must know that there is nothing higher and stronger and
> more wholesome and good for life in the future than some
> good memory, especially a memory of childhood, of home.
> People talk to you a great deal about your education, but
> some good sacred memory, preserved from childhood, is
> perhaps the best education. If a man carries many such mem-
> ories with him into life, he is safe to the end of his days. And
> if one has only one good memory left in one's heart, even that
> may sometime be the means of saving him.[19]

The old couple espied by Schmemann, the disconsolate lover
who falls into a "Gratitude Zone," the young boys to whom Karamazov is speaking, all bear witness in their different ways to the
mysterious presence that mediates the joy of Christ's death and
resurrection. His is the one "sacred memory" that is enough to
keep us to the end of our days, the one "sacred memory" that renders the ordinary gifts of life into mysterious signs of his presence.
Such signs refer us beyond ourselves to the Easter joy, which alone
can keep us from despairing when everything else in our life
argues that we should. Such joy is less an emotion we feel than it
is a "real presence" that indwells us and gives us to know, against
all evidence to the contrary, that life is a good gift whose goodness
is mysterious most of all to ourselves. Such a presence is not an
uplifting sense of well-being attainable only by the optimistic and

well-fixed, but a gift that emerges from the ordinary scenes of life—the way the beauty of a sunflower can overpower one's heart, the way a tree's branches claw after a winter sky, the way a smile pierces through a rainy day, the way a good weariness enfolds us at the close of a long day. Just so do these gifts become witnesses to that One whose passion transformed death to life.

But the "sacred memory" that sustains us in life is inseparable from the particular story of the God whose own life is not endless work 24/7, but whose Sabbath rest is instead the end and purpose of all creation. This, of course, is why Easter's great gift is the true meaning of Sabbath rest, the interruption of all our "dead certainties" by the risen Lord whose joy it is to be God with us. That is why the true home of joy, the place where it surprises us most of all, is in the praise and worship of that gathered community that lives from this Easter promise.

Karl Barth's *Church Dogmatics* has a section on "the meaning of Sunday freedom." We will look more closely at what he says concerning this freedom in chapter 5. Here it is enough to note that the joy of Sunday worship comes, Barth thinks, not from a commitment on our part to do something, much less to do nothing, but from the gift of the day itself, the way it interrupts our lives with its claims and so in its strangeness recalls us "to the great interruption of the everyday world by Easter Day."[20] The "meaning of Sunday freedom," Barth writes, "is joy, the celebrating of a feast."[21] Joy. It is the day of celebration in which we remember not what we have done but what God has done in the resurrection of Jesus Christ from the dead. Here too there is a risk, for we are quite capable of thinking such a feast of joy must mean that we must get busy and achieve sufficient levels of joyful activity. But Barth cautions against doing anything programmatic. Instead he talks about worship as the day of entering into God's joy in which the end and purpose of all creation is seen clearly in the feast laid out in Jesus Christ.

> The church must not allow itself to become dull, nor its services dark and gloomy. It must be claimed by, and proclaim, the lordship of God in the kingdom of his dear Son rather

than the lordship of the devil or capitalism or communism or human folly and wickedness in general. . . . Who otherwise will believe it when it says that the holy day is made the day of joy for men and therefore the day of God?[22]

This is the great gift of Sabbath: joy in Christ. This is "the joyful feast of the people of God." Here we eat God's word and celebrate the living Christ who refuses to leave us in darkness or abandon us to ourselves.

✠✠✠✠✠✠✠

The language of joy is often expressed better in poetry than in prose, which is one reason the psalms are so beloved by people of faith. It seems right, then, to conclude this first chapter on the joy of ministry with a poem about such joy by a minister. "The Bunch of Grapes" was written by George Herbert, a seventeenth-century poet who left the serious business of the academy and government to become a parish priest.[23]

Herbert thinks that joy finds us, just as he thinks that Scripture is the most profound interpreter of our lives. We tend to think that we find happiness, just as we tend to think (at least since Descartes) that we are the primary interpreters of our own lives and of Scripture. But Herbert thinks Scripture "reads" us and draws us into its world, from which perspective we begin to understand our own. In its light we see light.

Herbert believes that joy is the great gift of the gospel, but it is a gift that, like manna, cannot be turned into a commodity, something that can be bought or sold, or stored up for use for our own purposes. It remains ever a gift, for as we seek to make use of joy rather than receive it, we surely lose it, much as Jesus reminds us of the strange economy of God's grace, that as we seek to save our own lives we most surely lose them.

The Bunch of Grapes

Joy, I did lock thee up: but some bad man
Has let thee out again:

And now I am where I began
   Seven years ago: one vogue and vein,
   One air of thoughts usurps my brain.
I did toward Canaan draw; but now I am
Brought back to the Red Sea, the sea of shame.

For as Jews of old by God's command
   Traveled, and saw no town:
So now each Christian has his journeys measured:
   Their story pens and sets us down.
   A single deed is small renown.
God's works are wide, and set in future times;
His ancient justice overflows our crimes.

Then have we too our guardian fires and clouds;
   Our scripture-dew drops fast:
We have our sands and serpents, tents and shrouds;
   Alas! Our murmurings come not last.

   But where's the cluster? Where's the taste
Of mine inheritance? Lord, if I borrow,
Let me as well take up their joy, as sorrow.

But can he lack the grape, who has the wine?
   I have their fruit and more.
Blessed be God, who prospered Noah's vine,
   And made it bring forth grapes good store.
   But much more him I must adore,
Who of the law's sour juice sweet wine did make,
Even God himself, being pressed for my sake.

   The poem begins with the poet's admission that he sought to turn joy into his own private property, to lock it up and set it to his own use, perhaps even his own religious use. "But some bad man / Has let thee out again." Could it be that Herbert also believes that it is through the cross that joy comes and makes itself known precisely in resisting our efforts to commodify it, remaining ever a gift? In any case, in the economy of God's forgiveness, grace always occasions the discovery of our need of grace, of our being weak precisely at the point where we thought ourselves strongest. As a result Christian ministry is ever and always a beginning at the beginning, again and again. In this case, the poet returns to where he was seven years ago, perhaps at the beginning of his own ministry, but in any case not as one who now has it all together but as one who, having lost his way, has lost also the joy of following in this way. He returns to the point of his deliverance, employing the Old Testament image of Israel's salvation, the Red Sea, calling it the "sea of shame" not because he belittles what happened there but because the memory of what happened there so vividly reveals his own neediness.

The Christian's journey, Herbert insists, is best interpreted by Israel's journey, where one sees quite clearly what "wilderness wandering" really means. "Their story pens and sets us down," just as God's "ancient justice overflows our crimes." We too struggle to move forward and are able to do so only by such elusive yet steadfast signs as fire and cloud. Scripture itself becomes our manna, and in truth, "We have our sands and serpents, tears and shrouds." Indeed, perhaps nothing is more characteristic of our life together in the church than the fact that "our murmurings come not last."

Yet the poet knows there should be joy. The spies who ventured into the promised land did bring back a cluster of grapes, and if Israel's story really does interpret the Christian life, then where is our cluster? Where is the joy?

Joy, the poet suggests, is still in the grapes, the grapes that are always a sign of God's promise, the grapes that were crushed ("pressed") on the cross of Jesus Christ in order that there might indeed be wine for all who thirst. "For through the cross, joy came into the world." That is what is being carried on this piece of wood on which the spies hung the cluster of grapes, and that is what the cross bears in Jesus Christ, who is himself the "cluster of grapes" incarnate and "pressed" for our sake. Here is the gift of joy that resists all our efforts to turn it into something more "useful," even as it graciously invites us to taste and see the unbought and unbuyable goodness of its own wine. Here is the unlikely way joy enters the world, on a crossbar as a cluster of grapes, on the cross in Jesus Christ, around a table laden with bread and wine that calls itself a feast and invites all to come and eat.

Chapter Two

Dostoyevsky as an Apostle of Joy

Evangelion (that we call the gospel) . . . is a Greek word and signifieth good, merry, glad and joyful tidings, that maketh a man's heart glad, and maketh him sing, dance, and leap for joy.
—William Tyndale[1]

But we must also remember that the man who hears and takes to heart the biblical message is not only not permitted but plainly forbidden to be anything but merry and cheerful.
—Karl Barth[2]

I n his book *Under the Unpredictable Plant*, Eugene Peterson relates how he was mentored in his pastoral vocation by Fyodor Dostoyevsky.

I made several attempts to find a vocational mentor from the living, without success. Then I found Fyodor Dostoyevsky. I cannot now remember how I hit on him, for I had no previous acquaintance. An inspired hunch maybe. A whim that turned lucky. The more accurate, albeit antique, word is "providence."[3]

Peterson goes on to tell how he made regular "appointments" with Dostoyevsky, reading first from *The Idiot* and later from other novels and stories. Dostoyevsky's particular gift to Peterson was not a new pastoral strategy for getting things done or becoming a success, nor did he offer a comprehensive theory that would enable Peterson to explain things to his benighted parishioners. Indeed, the culture in which Peterson was attempting to pastor was already drowning in such explanations and only too happy to reduce the mysterious joy of the church's life to something more manageable and "productive." In contrast, Dostoyevsky provided the gift of a vision, a sanctified imagination that could sympathetically depict the messiness of human existence with all of its passions and painful contradictions while revealing in its very midst the even deeper mystery of a grace incarnate in the lives of these fictional characters. Peterson writes:

> Dostoyevsky's large-spirited, extravagant, and reckless immersion in the depths of evil and suffering, love and redemption, recovered God and passion for me. Stavrogin [a character in *The Devils*] was not a man who could be dissuaded from his evil life and educated into salvation with a newly revised church school curriculum. Alyosha did not become holy by attending a therapy group.[4]

It would be too much to say that *The Brothers Karamazov* is simply about joy. The novel is too full of characters, parables, and stories within the story to reduce to a single theme. Moreover, the narrative speaks of great human misery: the murder of a father, the suicide of a son, a trial in which another son is convicted falsely and sent to Siberia, the illness and death of a boy whose pathetic end frames the final part of the novel. This is not a novel about the adventures of a happy family who live out beautiful days in the neighborhood. It is full of bitterness, shame, despair, and defiant self-centeredness. Yet it is full of characters who amid great suffering come to know the deepest joy, and to that extent it is a story that offers what is rarely found in modern literature, a genuinely happy ending.

Dostoyevsky's most prominent biographer summarizes the novel as a "conflict between reason and faith," with faith understood as "the irrational core of the Christian commitment."[5] Yet such an assessment overlooks the novel's central conviction that only the love of God is able to redeem a broken world and that only as we come to know this love and recognize our place at its table are we made capable of love. This love of God for his creation, Dostoyevsky thinks, is the one true thing, more true than all of our theories or passions or failures. As Charles Taylor has pointed out, Dostoyevsky knows that given all of the evil and degradation that we ourselves and the world contain, to embark on any attempt to love this world (and ourselves) requires something of "a miracle."[6] But this miracle is precisely what the Holy Spirit offers to a modernity caught up in its own despairing boredom, and why such an unwanted and unexpected gift so often is characterized in terms of a liberation. This is the miracle to which the novel bears witness and which forms the core of its complicated and tangled story.

The gift of this miracle, however, is not just its liberating power but also its self-forgetting joy. "Hell," Father Zossima famously says in the novel, "is the suffering of being unable to love."[7] And what makes this suffering particularly hellish is the joyless inability to forget self. Even our various schemes of salvation do not liberate us from such a hell, for such schemes have at their center the self-justifying "I" whose tyranny oppresses even as it grows more religious. Joy, on the other hand, comes from outside ourselves and takes the form of a gift. Early in the novel, when the hero of the first half of the story, Father Zossima, is accused of being "happy," he replies, "You could never say anything that would please me more. For men are made for happiness, and anyone who is completely happy has a right to say to himself, 'I am doing God's will on earth.' All the righteous, all the saints, all the holy martyrs were happy."[8] Such happiness is the joy that is able, like the birds of the air and the lilies of the field, to praise God with unselfconscious gratitude.

Father Zossima is an elder, an old monk living in the hermitage of a monastery near the Karamazov estate. An elder, Dostoyevsky tells us, has no formal ecclesiastical office but is distinguished for his holiness, his saintly power to look into the depths of another person's soul and claim its gifts for God. As a person of such holiness, Father Zossima is widely sought after for pastoral advice, instruction, even blessings. So many people come to Father Zossima to confess their sins or entreat him for a word of grace that he is thought to be able to tell from a stranger's face the nature of his suffering or the content of his petition.

> Alyosha noticed that many, almost all, went in to the elder for the first time with apprehension and uneasiness, but came out with bright and happy faces. He was particularly struck by the fact that Father Zossima was not at all stern. On the contrary, he was almost gay. The monks used to say that he was more drawn to those who were more sinful, and the greater the sinner the more he loved him.[9]

In an early chapter in the novel, "Peasant Women Who Have Faith," Dostoyevsky offers three vignettes of Father Zossima's pastoral care in which joy emerges as the great gift of the gospel. This gift is not offered as a bromide nor merely as an exhortation to be cheerful. Rather, the joy that is offered by Father Zossima perceives and addresses great suffering, revealing itself to be no stranger to human misery but refusing to let such misery define the terms of a life that belongs to God.

The first vignette concerns a "crazy woman" who, when brought to Father Zossima, "began shrieking and writhing as though in pains of childbirth." Quietly, Father Zossima laid his stole on her forehead and read a prayer over her, "and she was at once soothed and quieted."[10]

The reader cannot help but see the Christlike nature of this exorcism. However, as the story makes clear, this is a real engagement with human misery. Dostoyevsky describes the suffering of such "possessed" women, who would bark like dogs during the mass but become quiet as the sacrament was brought in. Such women, Dostoyevsky tells us, were prevalent in Russia because of the suffering and hardship they faced. There was "the exhausting toil too soon after hard, abnormal, and unassisted labor in childbirth" and, worse, "the hopeless misery, from beatings" which many could not endure. Some might call it trickery, he acknowledges, but the sacrament's power to heal was unquestioned by those who supported the woman in anguish, and they believed "that the evil spirit in possession of her could not hold out if she were brought to the sacrament and made to bow down before it."[11] So it was when Father Zossima touched the sick woman with his stole.

Some might object that this form of pastoral care is nothing but a soothing piece of magic intended to pacify a troubled soul. Dostoyevsky himself admits that such exorcisms were often explained as "the trickery of the 'clericals.'" Still, as the story makes clear, even as the stole is laid on her forehead and Father Zossima reads a short prayer over her, what is recalled is the power of the sacrament to heal the wretched of the earth, that is, the power of Christ's own presence to redeem a broken and tormented world. Word and sacrament are at the heart of this story, and as Father Zossima offers them to the miserable, Christ's real presence takes her life into his own, rendering her "like a child quieted at its mother's breast."

The peasant women who witness this healing miracle respond to its evangelical grace as their New Testament counterparts responded to Jesus, that is, with great joy. They "were moved to tears of ecstasy" by this moment, with some trying to kiss the hem of Father Zossima's garment and others lifting up their voices in praise.[12]

In this scene as in all of these vignettes, it is important to see that Dostoyevsky portrays only hopeless cases. That is, none of these "healing miracles" are occasions of cheap grace or instant success or even hopeful progress. The misery we face, he thinks, cannot be fixed by a strategy or program. Indeed, he would agree with Auden that "nothing can save us that is possible."[13] That is what it means to live by grace. Moreover, Dostoyevsky knows what Simone Weil later observed about literature and morality. "Imaginary evil," she writes, is always "romantic and varied; (while) real evil is gloomy, monotonous, barren, boring. Imaginary good is boring; real good is always new, marvelous, intoxicating. Therefore 'imaginary literature' is either boring or immoral (or a mixture of both). It only escapes from this alternative if in some way it passes over to the side of reality through the power of art—and only genius can do that."[14] Dostoyevsky's genius is just that, namely, to be able to "pass over to the side of reality" and portray the monotonous, barren misery of true evil while narrating the fresh, joyful, entirely unsentimental beauty of true goodness, all in the same story and sometimes even in the same character. There is nothing more difficult for the fiction writer, Flannery O'Connor once pointed out, than "making good people believable."[15] But of course, such "realism" is what Scripture regularly narrates in its stories of Jacob and Joseph, Moses and David, Peter and Paul. It is not that easy to sentimentalize such characters, and it can be done only by steering clear of the text itself. Evil is never sentimentalized in Scripture but is presented as a persistent and oppressive shadow whose "impossibility" is only too real. Similarly, suffering is neither explicable nor particularly edifying (see the book of Job) but a mysterious burden that, though it has no final place in God's new creation ("Mourning and crying and pain will be no more," Rev. 21:4), can teach us things about Christ that we come to know in no other way.

In the second vignette, Dostoyevsky probes more deeply into the nature of this kind of suffering. A peasant woman whose three-year-old son has died approaches Father Zossima, weeping. She has already buried three children, but the death of this last one has withered her heart.

> I look at his little clothes, his little shirt, his little boots, and I weep. I lay out all that is left of him, all his little things. I look at them and weep. I say to Nikita, my husband, let me go on a pilgrimage. . . . My Nikita has begun drinking while I am away. . . . As soon as I turn my back he gives way to it. But now I don't think about him. It's three months since I left home. I've forgotten him. I've forgotten everything. I don't want to remember. . . . I'm through with him. I'm finished. . . . I don't want to look upon my house and my goods. I don't want to see anything at all.[16]

Father Zossima's first reply to this grief-stricken mother is to remind her that her child is even now singing with the angels in heaven. "Listen, mother," he says.

Once in olden times a holy saint saw in the Temple a mother like you weeping for her little one, her only one, whom God had taken. "Knowest thou not," said the saint to her, "how bold these little ones are before the throne of God? Verily there are none bolder than they in the Kingdom of Heaven. 'Thou didst give us life, O Lord,' they say, 'and scarcely had we looked upon it when Thou didst take it back again.' And so boldly they ask and ask again that God gives them at once the rank of angels. Therefore," said the saint, "thou too, O mother, rejoice and weep not, for thy little one is with the Lord in the fellowship of the angels."[17]

The mother listens to this and then sighs and says,

My Nikita tried to comfort with the same words as you. "Foolish one," he said, "why weep? Our son is no doubt singing with the angels before God." He says that to me but he weeps himself. I see that he cries like me. "I know, Nikita," said I. "Where could he be if not with the Lord God? Only he is not here with us as he used to be before." And if only I could look upon him once more, if only I could peep at him without going up to him, without speaking. . . . If only I could hear him pattering with his little feet about the room just once, . . . If only I could hear his little feet. . . . But he's gone, Father, he's gone, and I shall never hear him again. Here's his little sash, but him I shall never see or hear now.[18]

As she looks at the sash, she begins to shake with sobs, her hands covering her eyes, unable, however, to stanch the flow of tears. "It is Rachel of old," says the elder,

weeping for her children. And she will not be comforted because they are not. Such is the lot set on earth for you mothers. Be not comforted. Consolation is not what you need. Weep and be not consoled, but weep. . . . A long while yet will you keep that great mother's grief. But it will turn in the end into quiet joy. And your bitter tears will be only tears

of sorrow that purify the heart and deliver it from sin. And I
shall pray for the peace of your child's soul. . . . And I will also
pray for your husband's health. It is a sin for you to leave him.
Your little one will see from heaven that you have forsaken
his father and will weep over you. Why do you trouble his
happiness? He is living, for the soul lives forever, and though
he is not in the house, he is near you, unseen. How can he go
into the house when you say that the house is hateful to you?
To whom is he to go if you are not together, his father and
mother? He comes to you in dreams now, and you grieve. But
then he will send you gentle dreams. Go to your husband,
mother; go this very day.[19]

The grieving mother accepts this word and tells Father
Zossima, "Your words have touched my heart. . . . My Nikita,
my Nikita, you are waiting for me,"[20] she sings as she departs for
her home.

What is theologically interesting about this encounter is neither the initial comfort that is offered nor the resolution that
results in the return of the grieving mother to her home and husband, but Father Zossima's perception that lamentation is also an
act of faith, that it is a grieving appeal to God against God for a
gift that has been lost. In view of such a loss, it is entirely appropriate for the grieving heart to weep and to weep before God.
Moreover, any answer that is embarrassed by such tears or that
would seek to belittle or circumvent them with a solution would,
as the woman knows only too well, offer a comfort that is too
cheap. Yet even so, as Father Zossima makes clear, in not being
comforted such grief will always have to be on guard lest it too be
interrupted one day by a grace that is deeper than lamentation and
grief. The God before whom such lamentation is made is capable
of sending a stranger who will fall into step beside those who
grieve and turn their sorrow into joy. Indeed, that will happen,
Father Zossima insists, because grief is destined to be swallowed
up by joy—not replaced by joy, not distracted by joy, not entertained by joy, but comprehended by joy, such that in the measure
one grieves one comes to know an even deeper quiet joy.

The third vignette concerns an exhausted young peasant woman who is staring at Father Zossima in silence. When he asks her what she wants, she says, "I have sinned, Father. I am afraid of my sin."[21] The woman, who has traveled more than three hundred miles to see Father Zossima, tells him of her husband who used to beat her cruelly. Three years previously her husband had fallen ill, and as she watched him lying on his bed, she wondered if it would be better for her if he did not get well. In a low whisper, the woman confesses her sin to Father Zossima, and tells him that she has also confessed to her priest and been admitted to communion, but now she herself is ill and is afraid. Father Zossima responds:

> Fear nothing and never be afraid. And don't worry. If only your penitence fail not, God will forgive all. There is no sin and there can be no sin on all the earth, which the Lord will not forgive to the truly repentant! Man cannot commit a sin so great as to exhaust the infinite love of God. Can there be a sin which could exceed the love of God? . . . Believe that God loves you as you cannot conceive; that he loves you with your sin, in your sin. It has been said of old that over one repentant sinner there is more joy in heaven than over ten righteous men. Go, and fear not. Be not bitter against men. Be not angry if you are wronged. Forgive the dead man in your heart what wrong he did to you. Be reconciled with him in truth. If you are penitent, you love. And if you love, you are of God. All things are atoned for, all things are saved by love. . . . Love is such a priceless treasure that you can redeem the whole world by it, and cleanse not only your own sins but the sins of others.[22]

After saying these words to the woman, Father Zossima makes the sign of the cross over her and takes from his neck a small icon and puts it on her shoulders. "She bowed down to the earth without speaking."[23]

Father Zossima's words to the woman voice the deepest convictions of Dostoyevsky's own novelistic vision and summarize his understanding of redemptive love. "If I, a sinner even as you are," Father Zossima says to the woman, "am tender with you and have pity on you, how much more will God have pity on you."[24] The God with whom this peasant woman has to do is not a god who must be persuaded or harangued into forgiving; rather (how much more!), this God's mercy is what makes repentance possible at all, drawing sinners to the grace offered in the cross, whose sign is one of Father Zossima's gifts to the woman. There is where God's infinite love comprehends and overcomes our sin.

Moreover, this cross, far from being a sign of sorrow, is a sign of joy, the joy that is in heaven already, the joy that rejoices more over one penitent sinner than over ten righteous people. Indeed, this is how joy enters the world. For such joy is the gift of the cross and therefore the proper possession of every sinner. What Father Zossima seeks to offer in his pastoral care is not just forgiveness, not the squaring of some moral equation or even the reclamation of one who is "lost," but a redescription of who God is and how the terms of God's own life reconstitute our own. That is why, ultimately, a repentance that trusts in God's inconceivable grace has to be described in terms of joy, for that is what it means to receive the sign of the cross and to find one's life within its resurrection terms.

One other aspect of this story should not be missed. The peasant woman, after receiving Father Zossima's blessing, bows down to the earth. Often in this novel characters bow down to the earth or even kiss it.[25] For Dostoyevsky, joy is not some ethereal gift available only to those who are spiritually in touch with it. Joy is quite earthly, and to receive joy always entails embracing the earth, accepting one's creatureliness, and doing so not reluctantly or resignedly but with a grateful heart. Charles Taylor has suggested that grace in Dostoyevsky's novel is like a current flowing through the earth, the rejection of which always results in a loathing of what is earthly and ultimately in a kind of self-loathing. "Rejecting the world seals one's sense of its loathsomeness and of one's own, insofar as one is part of it. And from this can only come acts of hate and destruction."[26] Dostoyevsky's vision is deeply incarnational, which is why his most troubled characters are nearly always the most spiritual or intellectual or otherwise resentful of the limitations of their own humanity. The love that overcomes evil and makes sinners capable of love is, not surprisingly, always incarnate love and more often than not results in the recipient embracing the very earth from whose limits he or she previously sought escape. To love, for Dostoyevsky, always means to accept our being in this world and not to seek or even want a salvation apart from it.[27]

✥✥✥✥✥✥✥✥

The moral and theological center of Dostoyevsky's novel takes place in an extended conversation between two of the brothers, Ivan and Alyosha. For some interpreters, Ivan seems easily categorized as the embodiment of a modern rationalist, a good representative of the Enlightenment, a skeptic who enjoys pointing out the inconsistencies of faith. Yet such a picture of Ivan ignores the depths of his own struggle and the degree to which he takes God seriously, much more seriously, for example, than the other representatives of "Enlightened liberalism" who appear in the novel and for whom Dostoyevsky shows little interest. Ivan loves Alyosha and in many ways longs to believe as fervently and simply as his brother. Moreover, Ivan sees the implications of his own nihilism, and what he fails to see is brought home to him with painful clarity in the patricide-suicide of his half brother, Smerdyakov, who does the unpardonable by taking Ivan's philosophy seriously.

Ivan, in any case, is not an atheist. If he were, his agony would be merely a "problem." No, what Ivan rejects is not God but any notion of salvation that would justify or comprehend the suffering of innocent "little ones." In the chapter titled "Rebellion," Ivan rehearses for his brother, Alyosha, stories Dostoyevsky lifted from newspaper accounts of children who were abused, tortured, and killed. He begins with a story of Turkish soldiers tossing babies up in the air and catching them on their bayonets, of their holding a pistol for a child to play with and when he smiles, pulling the trigger in his face and blowing out his brains. Alyosha asks his brother what is the point of these stories, and Ivan replies only by telling worse stories of Europeans, of a Swiss boy, born illegitimate and abandoned by his parents, raised by shepherds who beat him, who later grew up to become a thief, killing a man in Geneva.

There good Swiss Calvinists taught him to read in prison and exhorted him to confess to the murder, which he eventually did, occasioning much rejoicing over his penitent heart, rejoicing that continued up to the point of his being guillotined.

This case "is interesting because it's national," Ivan continues. "Though to us it's absurd to cut off a man's head, because he has become our brother and has found grace, yet we have our own specialty, which is worse."[28] Ivan then rehearses what he considers the Russian penchant for beating animals, in this instance a peasant beating a dray horse, who dies after being lashed across the eyes, and who falls trembling under an impossible load. He tells of a little girl of five, the daughter of very cultivated parents who beat her incessantly, locking her up in a privy because she wet her bed, smearing her face and mouth with excrement.

> Can you understand why a little creature, who can't even understand what's done to her, should beat her little aching heart with her tiny fist in the dark and the cold, and weep her meek unresentful tears to dear, kind God to protect her? Do you understand that, Alyosha, you pious and humble novice? Do you understand why this infamy must be and is permitted? Without it, I am told, man could not have existed on earth, for he could not have known good and evil. Why should he know that diabolical good and evil when it costs so much? Why, the whole world of knowledge is not worth that child's prayer to "dear, kind God"![29]

Ivan concludes this harrowing series of cruelties with a story of a little boy of eight who had the temerity to throw a rock that injured the paw of a Russian general's dog. In consequence, the general decides to "hunt" the child, setting the pack of dogs after him until the boy is torn to pieces in front of his mother's eyes.

In acknowledging that he is using stories of children to make his point more vivid, Ivan concludes:

> Oh, Alyosha, I am not blaspheming! I understand, of course, what an upheaval of the universe it will be, when everything

in heaven and earth blends in one hymn of praise and everything that lives and has lived cries aloud: "Thou art just, O Lord, for Thy ways are revealed." When the mother embraces the fiend who threw her child to the dogs, and all three cry aloud with tears, "Thou art just, O Lord!" then, of course, the crown of knowledge will be reached and all will be made clear. But what troubles me is that I can't accept the harmony. . . . It's not worth the tears of that one tortured child who beat itself on the breast with its little fist and prayed in its stinking outhouse, with its tears to "dear, kind God"! . . . I don't want the mother to embrace the oppressor who threw her sons to the dogs! She dare not forgive him! Let her forgive him for herself, if she will. . . . But the sufferings of her tortured child she has no right to forgive; she dare not forgive the torturer, even if the child were to forgive him! . . . I don't want harmony. . . . Besides too high a price is asked for harmony; it's beyond our means to pay so much. And so, I give back my entrance ticket, and if I am an honest man I give it back as soon as possible. And that I am doing. It's not God that I don't accept, Alyosha, only I most respectfully return the ticket to him.[30]

To understand Alyosha's response to this, one must be clear about the nature of Ivan's "rebellion." In "returning his ticket" he is not rejecting God or even pointing out that the presence of suffering in the world raises questions about the moral intelligibility of the universe. No; what Ivan rejects is any notion of salvation that comprehends a world so constituted and so ordered that suffering can somehow be justified as part of the divine plan. As David Hart has pointed out, Ivan's particular complaint is not that of Voltaire, who gleefully pointed to the Lisbon earthquake of 1755 as proof that the ordered harmony of the Deists was a fraud. "Voltaire sees only the terrible truth that the actual history of suffering and death is not morally intelligible. Dostoyevsky sees— and this bespeaks both his moral genius and his Christian view of reality—that it would be far more terrible if it were. . . . After all, Ivan asks, if you could bring about a universal and final beatitude for all beings by torturing one small child to death, would you think the price acceptable?"[31] Ivan's refusal to let suffering be used to justify the ways of God, even to justify one's own salvation, is not only admirable but theologically profound. Yet in his desire to "return his ticket," one hears in Ivan's agony not a love for the miserable but a loathing of the earthly. It is Ivan's moral sensitivity that is offended, not his faith. Indeed, as has been pointed out by others, it is characteristic of Dostoyevsky's art that "the more noble and sensitive and morally insightful one is, the more one is liable to feel this loathing."[32] Rejecting the world offers a kind of moral protection, however illusory, from its degradation and filth. "We, at least, are not a part of *that*," one might say. And so it is that Ivan seeks to hold on to his integrity.

In response to Ivan's confession, Alyosha reminds him of Jesus, who, Alyosha says, "gave his innocent blood for all."[33] Ivan, however, has anticipated this response, and in reply relates to Alyosha his long prose poem "The Grand Inquisitor." In this poem, Jesus visits Seville during the Inquisition and is imprisoned there as a heretic and ultimately exiled because the church cannot abide his presence. Before leaving the city, however, Jesus turns to the Grand Inquisitor, who longs for him to say something bitter and terrible, if for no other reason than to prove that the Inquisitor's power was at least capable of provoking Jesus' wrath, and instead kisses the old man on his forehead. That is Jesus' answer.

Having listened to Ivan's parable, Alyosha turns to his brother, who wants so badly to hold himself apart from the loathsome misery of this world, and kisses him on the forehead. "That's plagiarism,"[34] Ivan cries, as indeed it is. But that is all Alyosha has to offer his very spiritual and intellectually acute brother, who sees so clearly the cruel injustice of the world and is determined not to be contaminated by it, much less accept responsibility for it. Ivan in this sense is a "schismatic"[35] who has separated himself from the world. Alyosha's response to such morally sensitive wisdom is a kiss, a form of joyful embrace that embarrasses and scandalizes Ivan as much as the gospel's embrace of a sinful and messy world. Such a kiss implies that the only faithful response to Ivan's agony is to point to the miracle of Jesus Christ. It seems silly, if not stupid, to say that Jesus is the answer, and indeed, Jesus is not the answer to so many of the things one might desire. But to one whose sensitivity to the world's injustice is so acute that a prideful "schism" is the only conceivable response to its pain, the miracle and mystery of him who "though he was in the form of God" became flesh "even to death on the cross" describe the God who refuses to be "schismatic" about this world and who insists on kissing it with his life. Alyosha's kiss, like Jesus' in Ivan's parable of the Grand Inquisitor, bears witness to the gospel's unflappable, incorrigible, marvelously earthly joy.

The Brothers Karamazov ends with a word of praise for a name—Karamazov—that is as messy and dirty and scandalous as any could be, a name that has been dragged through the courts, through various separations, acts of greed and violence and despair, but which in the end receives this joyful "Yes!" "Hurrah for Karamazov," the group of boys cry. What occasions this cheer is a sermon given to these twelve little boys (apostles?) by Alyosha, memorializing and celebrating the life of one of their companions. Alyosha on this occasion is asked, "Can it be true as they teach us in church, that we shall all rise again from the dead and shall live and see each other again, all, Ilusha too?" And Alyosha replies with the joyful simplicity and simple joy of the gospel: "Certainly we shall all rise again, certainly we shall see each other and shall tell each other with joy and gladness all that has happened!"[36] That word is what occasions the cheering, and that word is what binds earth to heaven in the joy of God.

Chapter Three

Laughing through the Tears
Joy and the Church's Theological Task

If you have heard the Easter message, you can no longer run around with a tragic face and lead the humorless existence of a man who has no hope. One thing still holds, and only this one thing is really serious, that Jesus is the Victor. A seriousness that would look back past this, like Lot's wife, is not a Christian seriousness. It may be burning behind—and truly it is burning—but we have to look, not at it, but at the other fact, that we are invited and summoned to take seriously the victory of God's glory in this man Jesus and to be joyful in him.

—Karl Barth[1]

Those who have hope of Christ only in this life cannot laugh (cf. I Cor. 15:19).

—Karl Barth[2]

In 1966, on the occasion of his eightieth birthday, Karl Barth received a Festschrift from his friends and former students titled *Parrhesia: Fröhliche Zuversicht.*[3] The "boldness of speech" indicated in this title by the Greek word *parrhesia* is translated by the German words for "happy confidence," all suggesting the joyful splendor of Karl Barth's theological vision. The passion with which Barth undertook the theological task was something that was noted by more than just his former students. In 1959, a lead story about this Swiss theologian appeared in the German news magazine *Der Spiegel* with the headline "A joyful partisan of the good God."[4] Nine years later, at the memorial service in Basel celebrating Barth's life and witness, Eberhard Jüngel, representing the younger generation of theologians, had this to say about his mentor: "Barth's theology reflects joy, indeed, delight in knowing. He was in no way of the opinion that we are able to know nothing; even less did he think that we are able to know everything. His faith sought understanding: '*Fides quarens intellectum*,' the title he gave to his favorite book [on Anselm]. . . . His thought and his life were the collaborative effort to indicate that 'God' is a delightful word."[5]

Taking delight in God has not always been the way theologians have described their task, nor is it the only way Barth's own theology has been construed.[6] One theologian who recognized immediately the importance of joy and delight in Barth's understanding of theology was his Swiss neighbor, the Roman Catholic theologian Hans Urs von Balthasar. The reason to read Barth, von Balthasar suggests, is that

> his theology is lovely. I do not mean merely that stylistically Barth writes well, though he does. But the beauty of his prose emerges more because he unites two things: passion and impartiality. He is passionately enthusiastic about the subject matter of theology, but he is impartial in the way he approaches so volatile a subject. Impartiality means being plunged into the object, the very definition of objectivity. And Barth's object is God, as he has revealed himself in Jesus Christ, to which revelation scripture bears witness. . . . Barth focuses on the Word, fully and exclusively, that its full splendor might radiate out to the reader. Who but Barth has gazed so breathlessly and tirelessly on his subject, watching it develop and blossom in all its power before his eyes? . . . Barth really makes us believe that for him Christianity was a radiantly triumphant opportunity. He manages this, not so much because he possesses the gift of style or writes well, but because he bears witness, sober witness, to a reality that epitomizes style, since God is its author.[7]

Similarly, Dietrich Bonhoeffer, writing to Eberhard Bethge from Tegel Prison in Berlin, used the word *hilaritas* to describe the zest with which Barth undertook the theological task.[8] Theology, as Barth understood it, could manifest a "high-spirited self-confidence," not because of some bravado or overbearing ego on the part of the theologian but because, without our permission or help, God has spoken and in Jesus Christ has said Yes to all creation. This christological Yes is the basis of everything theology has to say, and it enables theology itself to become truly articulate.

This Yes is also what makes theology a deeply joyful enterprise, whose work derives not from the theologian's commitment to the transcendence of God but from the scandalous intimacy of God's self-giving. Joseph Mangina has noted how Barth's view of theology differs at this point from Protestant liberals like Paul Tillich and H. Richard Niebuhr, both of whom were concerned to protect the transcendence of God by protesting any effort to elevate some part of creation to ultimate status.[9] Their fear was the historically Protestant, even Calvinistic fear of the sin of idolatry, a fear that recognizes the human propensity to manufacture idols out of our own desires, especially our nationalistic or religious desires. This propensity is resisted by asserting God's transcendence over any penultimate loyalty, reserving for God alone our worship and allegiance. As a result, theology undertaken in this way sees its primary task as protecting God's transcendence, emphasizing the distance between our concepts and God's reality. The theologian understands himself as the prophetic-critic here, the judge whose task is to remind us that God's ways are not our ways.

As Mangina notes, there is much in Barth's theology, especially in his early work, that is sympathetic to this emphasis on God's transcendence. But there are significant differences.

> The God of the Protestant principle tends to lack the concreteness and terrible intimacy of Barth's God, who distinguishes himself from the idol not, in the end, by being transcendent, but by becoming incarnate in Jesus Christ. . . . For Barth it is not finally the human subject who exercises

critique, but God who criticizes—or in biblical terms, judges—the world in Christ's cross and resurrection. Moreover, even this act of judgment is at its heart an affirmation. Both the substance and the overall tenor of Christian theology are governed by the triumphant "Yes" of God, making it a joyous exploration of God's ways in light of the accomplished (but at the same time ever new and fresh) action of God in Jesus Christ.[10]

Because God has drawn so intimately near, how could knowledge of this God be anything else but "the most thankful and happy science"?[11]

Since faith derives its life from God who is revealed in Jesus Christ, theological reflection is liberated from preoccupation with itself, Barth thinks, and set free to join with all of creation in the praise and service of God. The birds of the air and the lilies of the field, the angels and even smallest of creatures commit doxology every day, participating in their own way in the joy of knowing God. Their confident good cheer in response to God's gracious self-articulation makes our efforts to speak of God as if God were silent appear grimly wrongheaded if not perverse. Indeed, how can one even wish to reopen the abyss that God has already spanned in Jesus Christ, or prefer the silence to the Word God has voiced? A silent or distant god will always need our help to be brought to speech, which is why theologians who are often modest in their claims about our knowledge of God have no trouble seeing themselves at the center of the theological task. However, that way of doing theology, Barth thinks, results in a conversation in which the theologian is the only speaker.[12] This monologue is what has made so much of modern theology such a joyless enterprise and why it appears to be either deaf or hopelessly self-absorbed. In contrast, Barth argues, theology is really not speech about God so much as it is human thought and words "directed toward God," responding to God's Word with our own, even daring to speak of God as "You," which makes of theology "a liturgical act," even a form of prayer.[13] Having said that, Barth does not think piety is a substitute for study or that theology is in any sense a private matter. The

Church Dogmatics is amazingly catholic in the breadth of its listening to the whole church's response to God's speaking, even engaging in conversation with those outside the church. Barth is, among other things, an impressive listener who is suspicious of our self-sufficiencies, especially those theological ones that require no miracle, no gift of the Holy Spirit, nothing as ordinary as bread and wine or as entangling as life together in the church or as hard as careful study and preparation. Moralistic, therapeutic, political, religious, or theoretical prophylactics that seek to keep theology "safe" by keeping God transcendently silent eventually silence theology as well, rendering it entirely self-referential, unable to rejoice in the God who has spoken and, indeed, who speaks and whose word graciously enables us to find our voices.

One way to think of Barth's theology is to view his work as an attempt to recover the splendor of the theological task, indeed, to recover its voice in the life of the church. He does this not with some theoretical construct nor by placing the theologian at the center of this undertaking but by taking seriously the church's own task of proclamation. Theology becomes a joyful undertaking as it serves the church in the task of preaching. Barth makes it clear that if the church had no commission to proclaim the gospel, there would be no need of theology at all. "Proclamation is essential, dogmatics is needed only for the sake of it."[14] The glory of theology, in this sense, consists in the unspectacular task of assisting those who regularly invite their fellow believers to "hear the word of God." In testing the church's words by the Word of the gospel, theology claims no access to a higher gnosis, no mastery of spiritual or intellectual techniques, no morally superior standing. It can only think with the church as it engages in the task of hearing and proclaiming the Yes that God has spoken. As difficult or contemptible or impractical as it might seem to us, the gospel of the God who says Yes in Jesus Christ is not ashamed to use the proclamation of sinners to get itself heard in the world. The church lives or dies by the word it hears and proclaims.

But just so, preaching is not a neutral thing, much less a matter of virtuosity or piety or knowledge. Because it is not merely a conversation with itself but is rather an act called into existence by

God's Word summoning believers to hear and speak faithfully, preaching is a form of discipleship, and therefore subject to the very Word it seeks to proclaim. Theology is what happens when the church reflects on the word it has heard and is charged to proclaim, asking to what extent its own proclamation corresponds to the story of Jesus Christ as attested in Scripture. That is why Barth thinks theology is both a humble and joyous task; it does not have to be more than it is. It does not attempt the impossible task of bringing God down to us. Nor does it bore us with talk of its own experience or expertise. It is entirely focused on the God whose Yes is unashamed of our humanity and who, in assuming our sinful flesh, not only reveals the stupidity of our efforts to inflate ourselves but, even more marvelous to relate, reveals the splendor of God's use of human speech to proclaim the gospel "like a king through the mouth of his herald."[15] Such a possibility seems, if anything, even more unlikely than the scandal of God in the flesh of the Crucified, but here the scandal of the cross reveals and confirms the equally disturbing scandal of the church's proclamation and the way God's Word unashamedly chooses to make use of our own.

That preaching no longer strikes many as the scandalous center of the church's work today indicates how far we have traveled from Barth's theology and perhaps also what a failure of nerve we have suffered in seeking to water down the claims of the gospel to meet modern sensibilities. In any case, for Barth the joy of ministry is deeply connected to the church's task of preaching, whose service of bearing witness to the Word made flesh is what gives rise to theology in the first place and makes of it such a joyful undertaking.

Prior to the revolutionary turn Barth and his fellow pastor and friend Edward Thurneysen sought to make in the early part of the last century, the task of theology was considered neither particularly joyous nor daring but a task that could be ventured as respectable only by speaking not of God but rather of ourselves.[16] This was the answer proposed for theology by Schleiermacher in response to the Enlightenment's rejection of revelation as "privileged" information inaccessible to human reason. At first glance, this proposal seems appealingly modest—to confine talk about God to the universal possibilities accessible to human religious experience, fitting God into our world, so to speak. But in truth, such "modesty" conceals an arrogance that assumes a God who is silent, even unknowable, confirming the human subject and humankind's religious and moral sensibilities as the center of all talk of God.

Such a way of doing theology, Barth thought, avoided the problem, indeed, invited theology to commit a kind of suicide.[17] Moreover, such a reduction can maintain itself only by ignoring the obstinate miracle of God's living presence in Jesus Christ. It does, however, have one advantage: a more distant god, particularly one who remains silent, would never embarrass us by speaking to us, but would be content to leave us to our own devices. Yet the God of Jesus Christ speaks and, in speaking, summons us to respond even as his word reveals that we are unable to say anything on our own. We ought, Barth thought, not to flee from our embarrassment but to name it "and by that very recognition give God the glory."[18] At least that way, theology, if it is done at all, is undertaken on the basis of God's self-giving, a doxological celebration of God's abundance in providing us, manna-like, words to say that are adequate to this miraculous gift. To rely on our own piety or virtuosity would be to starve to death. That is why the robust affirmation of the Blumhardts—"Jesus is Victor"— remained so important for Barth throughout his life and why such distinguished liberals as Harnack or brilliant exegetes as Bultmann remained baffled by Barth's devotion to these strange, almost New Testament, evangelists of the kingdom of God.[19]

And that is why later in his *Church Dogmatics* Barth would insist that Mozart has a place in Christian theology, because better than so many fathers of the church, Mozart knew "something about creation in its total goodness,"[20] a goodness that is no stranger to suffering and evil and even death but which does not allow them to have undisputed sway. Unlike the equilibrium of "the great theologian Schleiermacher—a matter of balance, neutrality and, finally, indifference," something else happens in the music of Mozart. "What occurs in Mozart is rather a glorious upsetting of the balance, a turning in which the light rises and the shadows fall, . . . in which joy overtakes sorrow without extinguishing it, in which the Yea rings louder than the ever-present Nay."[21] Mozart "neither needed nor desired to express or represent himself, his vitality, sorrow, piety, or any program. He was remarkably free from the mania of self-expression."[22] For Mozart, as for theology that seeks to reflect faithfully on the gospel of Jesus Christ, the

> sun shines but does not blind, does not burn or consume. Heaven arches over the earth, but it does not weigh it down, it does not crush or devour it. Hence earth remains earth, with no need to maintain itself in a titanic revolt against heaven. Granted, darkness, chaos, death, and hell do appear, but not for a moment are they allowed to prevail.[23]

The Yes rings louder than the still-existing No. Theology's task, Barth thought, was to hear that Yes, in all its affirmation, which means to hear also the No this Yes reveals, but to hear it not as some equal or independent negative, but only as the impossible note that does not belong in the chord which the Yes mysteriously comprehends and resolves. Joy is the major note; the light shines in the darkness, but the darkness cannot master it.

✢✢✢✢✢✢✢✢✢

In *Church Dogmatics* II/1, Barth considers God's attributes or perfections. In the course of considering God's glory, he asks whether it can be said that God is beautiful.

God is glorious. For Barth, this is not a self-evident fact but is derived from God's self-declaration in Jesus Christ, which means that God's glory is not the glory of some absolute transcendence but the radiance of God's presence as it reaches us in Jesus Christ and renders God knowable to us. God's self-giving is never given in vain.

> It is not the presence of a cold confrontation. It is not a presence which leaves blind eyes blind or deaf ears deaf. It is a presence that opens them. . . . God's glory is the indwelling joy of His divine being which as such shines out from Him,

which overflows in its richness, which in its super-abundance
is not satisfied with itself but communicates itself. . . . All
God's works must be understood . . . from this point of view.
All together and without exception they take part in the
movement of God's self-glorification and the communica-
tion of His joy.[24]

Barth is aware of the dangers of reducing God's glory to our
notions of beauty, of reducing theology to a form of aestheticism,
which would attempt to bring our understanding of God under
the control of human categories. Moreover, he admits that
"beauty" is not a major category on the order of "grace" or "holiness" or "eternity" in describing God's being. It can only be a sub-
category of "glory." Yet Scripture witnesses to the joy that God's
glory radiates in God's act of being gracious, merciful, patient, and
full of love. Indeed, Scripture talks without embarrassment of the
pleasure, the desire, the enjoyment that God's self-declaration
evokes from God's people. Can one know such joy apart from a
beauty that is beautiful in its delightful "uselessness"? Why is it
not enough to speak of God's grace in terms of its effectiveness or
in terms of the gratitude, awe, and obedience it evokes? Why does
knowledge of God yield such joy? Why such delight? Why is the
gospel incapable of being merely prosaic? Why do the psalms sing
their joy?

Barth answers that God's glory awakens joy in us because joy
"is something in God, the God of all perfections, which justifies
us in having joy, desire, and pleasure towards Him, which indeed,
obliges, summons, and attracts us to do this." This joy within
God is not derivable from our notions of beauty, but God's glory
radiates joy that is "also" beautiful. Without beauty, delight,
even splendor, God's glory "might well be joyless" and soon grow
"tedious and therefore finally neither persuasive nor convincing."[25] Still, it is God who must teach us what beauty is.

God teaches us about his beauty in three ways, Barth suggests.
The first has to do with God's self-declaration, which is persuasive and convincing not because it measures up to our standards
of what is persuasive and convincing but because in radiating joy

God gives himself to us in such a way that this gift "releases pleasure, desire, and enjoyment," so persuading and convincing us in
the very act of making himself known.[26] To know God is to rejoice
in God, to receive the delight that is God's presence. That is God's
beauty. Knowledge of God that is joyless is not knowledge of the
God to whom Scripture bears witness.

Second, the triune life of God "is radiant, and what it radiates
is joy. . . . It is, therefore, beautiful." To be sure, it is not the three-
ness or some triadic form that renders God beautiful but the life
of the Father, Son, and Holy Spirit whose joyful unity and dis-
tinctive harmony constitute the secret of God's beauty. "If we deny
this, we at once have a God without radiance and without joy (and
without humor!); a God without beauty."[27] The triune God is
"also" beautiful, rendering "God" a delightful word.

Third, the beauty of God is revealed in the incarnation. As the
center of all God's ways and works, the Son "reveals the beauty of
God in a special way and in some sense to a supreme degree."[28]
The beauty of the triune God, the joy which this God's self-
declaration evokes, the splendor of this God's glory, all of this
would have remained hidden and unknown to us had not the Word
become flesh in Jesus Christ. This is the miracle of all miracles, the
place where God draws near to us and gives himself to us most intimately. God's glory is distinguished from that of all other gods in
the intimate condescension with which God assumes the flesh of
sinful humanity, suffers the judgment that rightly should fall on us,
and clothes us with the holiness and righteousness that rightly
belong to God. Barth calls this exchange the "perfect fellowship"
established in Jesus Christ in which "God could not be more glorious," arousing joy in the unparadoxical, undialectical gift of
himself as the incarnate Word, neither a prisoner of his own transcendence nor a sentimental captive to our desires.[29]

Barth's doctrine of reconciliation does not appear until volume
4 of the *Church Dogmatics*, but one can find it in abbreviated form
here in his discussion of God's glory. The "beautiful in God's being,
that which stirs up joy" is God's being God in the flesh "without
confusion or alteration, yet also without separation or division."
This unity and distinction, this rest and movement reflect the tri-

une life of God who is "not only the source of all truth and all goodness, but also the source of all beauty."[30] But just as the divinity of Christ will be revealed in "the Lord as servant," so here his particular beauty is to be seen in the way the high and holy God turns toward us and stoops in love and faithfulness to draw us to himself. This is the way of the cross. Indeed, Barth cites Isaiah 53 to show to what extent the "beauty of Christ" is not simply a celebration of an aesthetically pleasing image. "If the beauty of Christ is sought in a glorious Christ who is not crucified, the search will always be in vain."[31] In the Christ of whom Scripture testifies, however, God's beauty will always embrace "death as well as life, fear as well as joy, what we might call the ugly as well as what we might call the beautiful. It reveals itself . . . in the turning from the self-humiliation of God for the benefit of man to the exaltation of man by God and to God. This turning is the mystery of the name of Jesus Christ and of the glory revealed in this name."[32]

Barth concludes this examination of God's glory by noting that it is not exhausted in its own brilliance; it awakens a glorification on the part of all creation. God's joy does not leave itself without witness and is not ashamed to dwell within and shine through the creaturely joy it awakens. Barth describes the particular glory or beauty of creaturely joy in terms of gratitude. He notes that the joy the creature feels in the face of God's glory is not something that is mandated, as if the creature were ordered to be joyful. Rather, in giving himself in love to the creature, God sets the creature free to correspond in joy and gratitude, making the creature, as the Heidelberg Catechism says, "wholeheartedly willing and ready from now on to live for him."

How does this happen? Where is the place of joy and gratitude? Barth's answer at first glance may seem surprising or even deflating, yet it is gloriously unspiritual in its simple celebration of the congregation:

> It is as we are gathered to the Church, as the Word is proclaimed to us, as we believe and profess our faith, as theology does it work, as all this being and action is a single prayer and yet also in particular presents itself before God as prayer,

that we really glorify God and therefore share in his self-glorification. . . . We may not be sad but glad to be in the Church, to hear the proclamation of the Word, to respond in faith to this proclamation of God, to confess this faith, seriously to present this profession in theology. We may be glad to pray. The whole energy of the awakening and calling of the creature to its destiny to give glory to God works itself out here and now, wholly and utterly in the fact that the Church may be.[33]

A strange place, one might think, to seek or to find the beauty of God, that is, in the gathered fellowship of a not self-evidently beautiful collection of sinners. Yet where else would the God who elects to be glorious in the crucified and risen Lord be confessed and known, except as the head of such a questionable body with such dubious charms? Here is a strange glory indeed, one that is not paradoxical or ironic but almost irresponsibly fleshly, a glory that sings of the Lord who refuses to be without his own *glorious* people—not, to be sure, his perfect or flawless or even faithful people, but glorious in that they belong to this Lord who chooses to be glorious among them and in that way glorious in all the world.

The argument of this book is that the joy that sustains ministry is inseparable from the joy that Jesus Christ evokes as God in the flesh. The church has always been tempted to disbelieve its own glory, indeed, to take its own brokenness or miserable failures more seriously than the glory of its life in the crucified and risen Lord. That is why the church has always found the Gnostic option so appealing. The fleshliness of the church so often appears contemptible, and the prospect of a cleaner, more "spiritual" or intellectual existence is so compelling that we soon come to despise the smallness and ineffectual nature of congregational life, preaching, study, service, prayer. These hardly seem to be the things of glory and, in view of the world's miseries, are pitifully incommensurate with the need.

Which is why in the midst of his discussion of God's glory, Barth dares to talk about the "uselessness" of theology, a uselessness manifest in its peculiar beauty that refuses to be "used" but can only give delight. The terms he uses are at least as old as Augustine,[34] but the joy he espies he confesses to have learned from Anselm.

> At this point we may refer to the fact that if its task is correctly seen and grasped, theology as a whole, in its parts and in their interconnection, in its content and method, is, apart from anything else, a peculiarly beautiful science. Indeed, we can confidently say that it is the most beautiful of all the sciences. To find the sciences distasteful is the mark of the Philistine. It is an extreme form of Philistinism to find, or to be able to find, theology distasteful. The theologian who has no joy in his work is not a theologian at all. Sulky faces, morose thoughts and boring ways of speaking are intolerable in this science. May God deliver us from what the Catholic Church reckons one of the seven sins of the monk— *taedium*—in respect of the great spiritual truths with which theology has to do. But we must know, of course, that it is only God who can keep us from it.[35]

Why is theology so beautiful? One might think that the answer would be simply because its object is so glorious. But Barth is making more than just an aesthetic point. "Indeed, we can confidently say that it is the most beautiful of all the sciences." It is part of the beauty of theology (and therefore of preaching and ministry) that it is confident, not defiant or argumentative but quietly confident that in doing its work it is offering to the world something splendid, even beautiful. The *taedium* that Barth suggests is a threat to those in ministry is the despair, the sloth, that has become bored with wonder, unfazed by the miraculous, unaccountably weary with God's self-giving grace.

These sins do not afflict just those who enter the ministry. They have accompanied God's people throughout their history, from the children of Israel whose feet were scarcely dry when they asked

Moses what God had done for them lately, to the Corinthian church unimpressed with Paul's "more excellent way" of love. No doubt this sin of despair, even self-contempt, is but another form of pride that will do anything, even cling to its own "tragic" resignation, to avoid having to deal with the unsettling joy of God's relentless self-giving. Those who are charged to tell of this joy are particularly vulnerable to this sin of despair.

The church is easy to despise. Its failures are so dispiriting, its victories so small, its betrayals so disheartening. We look for signs of encouragement and settle for signs of success, particularly in numbers, and then despair when we do not see them or see only increasing loss and deeper fragmentation. Still, none of these things would overwhelm if there were not a deeper, underlying loss of joy. Smallness of size is no barrier to joy. Israel's history proves that. How many families look back on their history, starting out struggling to pay bills and caring for children and making a home, and remember not nostalgically but truly the joy of that struggle? A church battered by the culture, facing divisions within itself, unclear as to how the future will unfold can, nevertheless, know great joy in the struggle to bear witness to the victory of Jesus Christ. The often-unnoted secret of so many who courageously engaged in the civil rights struggle in the South in the 1950s and '60s was the joy they knew in risking their lives for something that mattered. Do we not at times envy them now?

Only the Holy Spirit, Barth writes, can deliver us from the tedium of being bored in the presence of God's grace—that is, the joy of knowing God requires a miracle, just as knowing God requires God's illuminating Spirit. It is one of the gifts of the Spirit to help us see that joy and to know from whence it comes. Theology can be beautiful and confident because God is faithful and is determined that nothing should take away the joy that is ours in Jesus Christ (John 16:22). Not even our self-assessment, not even our boredom and despair, nothing can take away this joy.

Barth returns to his mentor, Anselm, and notes that Anselm did not undertake the theological task in order to offer the church something merely useful. Theology, Anselm thought, was too beautiful for that. It was to be undertaken, at least in part, out of sheer delight in the beauty of its subject matter. The theology that dares to undertake this task will always reflect the confidence that rightly corresponds to the extravagant self-giving of the God who summons us to seek understanding of what we believe. The "peculiarly beautiful science" of theology draws upon the splendor of its subject matter to present to the world something beautiful, something excellent, something that the world cannot give to itself but can only receive with gratitude and praise. This is the *hilaritas*, the *parrhesia*, the happy confidence that ever accompanies those whose comfort it is to belong not to themselves but to their faithful Savior Jesus Christ.

Chapter Four

Joy Obscured

Gnosticism's Resentment of God's Particular Gifts

> When Emerson decided, in 1832, that he could no longer
> celebrate the Lord's Supper unless the bread and wine were
> removed, an important step in the vaporization of religion in
> America was taken, and the spirit of that step has continued
> apace. When the physical fact is separated from the spiritual
> reality, the dissolution of belief is eventually inevitable.
>
> Flannery O'Connor[1]

In chapter 2, we looked to Fyodor Dostoyevsky's novel *The
Brothers Karamazov* for what it might teach us about the nature
of ministry. In this chapter, we return to that novel to see what it
has to say about how the joy of ministry is subverted and what
resources exist for its recovery.

The Brothers Karamazov is a novel whose narrative twists and
turns entangle a host of characters and depict their struggles with
each other and with God. It has not always been interpreted as a
novel about ministry, though in many ways it is. Indeed, one can
make a case that this novel is about doxology, that is, what it means
to lift up one's heart in praise and gratitude to God. Many of the
crises in the characters' lives are precipitated by human failings:
illicit love affairs, calculating greediness, self-centered indifference, religious pride, cowardice, lust, murder, and suicide. Yet all
of these crises are portrayed as theological in nature, and most of

them implicitly or explicitly deal with a form of heresy that first emerged as critical in the second century of the church's life, Gnosticism.

Gnosticism hardly seems a threat today; the very word is redolent of dusty tomes of ancient history. Yet in recent years it has become widely used to explain certain aspects of contemporary culture.[2] In any case, Dostoyevsky clearly thought that at the heart of modernity's discontents was a kind of gnostic longing to escape the limits of embodied existence and to find a salvation unencumbered by time, place, or the constraining ties of circumstance. His objection to this counterfeit faith is not its heretical views or even its preoccupation with self but rather its resentment of the ordinary grace of life, a resentment that obscures from its adherents the joy of coming to know themselves as creatures of God. "Hell," he has Father Zossima say, "is the suffering of being unable to love."[3] That is the hell that afflicts the anguished souls whose contempt for this world's injustices (and whose loathing of themselves) renders them unable to participate in the joy and praise of God. It is worth attending to what Dostoyevsky thinks is so enticing and finally enslaving in this ancient and modern form of captivity and to see what liberating measures he thinks the gospel provides. If his vision is at all true, then nothing threatens to obscure from us the joy of ministry more than such contempt for the ordinary and quite fleshly means of grace that mediate God's gift of himself in Jesus Christ.

What is Gnosticism? As the early church encountered it, Gnosticism was a many-headed adversary, at once intensely religious and philosophically sophisticated, both parasitically attached to Christianity yet full of its own vocabulary and quite able to stand on its own. Its salient characteristics included (1) the positing of a radical dualism between God and the world, in which God is so utterly transcendent to the created order as to be literally inconceivable, and creation is the work of a lesser (and less gifted) Demiurge (the creator god); (2) a preoccupation with one's own salvation, the nature of which is "known" either by some secret knowledge or by private revelation; (3) a recognition that salvation of the soul requires escape from the imprisoning constraints of the body; (4) a solitary, even narcissistic concentration on self as a religious project in which the "other" is unnecessary; and (5) a rejection of the ordinary and external forms of faith, to be replaced by an "authentic" and even spiritually elite form of enlightenment.[4]

Gnostic elements appear in a variety of contemporary religious alternatives, such as the Church of Scientology and the teachings of Mary Baker Eddy's Christian Science, but what is striking about this set of characteristics is how pervasive they are throughout our culture. One example is "Sheila," in Robert Bellah's study of American life, *Habits of the Heart*, who describes her faith as "Sheilaism": "I believe in God. . . . I can't remember the last time I went to church. My faith has carried me a long way. It's Sheilaism. Just my own little voice."[5] More recently, the premise of the *Da Vinci Code* hinged on the importance of "secret knowledge" covered up by the fools or knaves of institutional and communal faith. Or, perhaps one thinks of Robert Putnam's study of the breakdown of community in American life in his book *Bowling Alone*.[6] All of which helps one understand why Harold Bloom has called Gnosticism "The American Religion."[7]

Two other characteristics of Gnosticism, manifest in both the ancient and modern varieties, are worth mentioning. The first is its expansiveness. It loves to explain things and is almost gaseous in its enveloping theories. It thrives in an information age that enables a virtual (and disembodied) reality and relies on the expertise, or celebrity, of elite virtuosos. At the same time it is suspicious of the particular, the embodied, the located, the time bound. It offers liberation from such intractable things. It lives, as Irenaeus, one of the first Christian critics of Gnosticism, noted, for its theories.[8]

The second characteristic, and one that is in many ways the other side of its expansiveness, is its loneliness. For the gnostic, the individual confronts the cosmos alone, and the salvation that is on offer is an intensely personal journey of self-discovery, cut off from any community or creedal faith. "Imagine a world without limits," a commercial importuned not so long ago, which at first hearing may seem attractive. Yet a world without limits runs roughshod over things like marriages, families, neighborhoods, congregations, and communities. The loneliness of so much of our present-day culture is a testimony to the continuing gnostic desire for a "world without limits."

How does Dostoyevsky help us see this threat, and what resources does he identify for combating it?

The hero of the first part of *The Brothers Karamazov* is Father Zossima, the beloved mentor of Alyosha (the hero of the second half of the novel). Shortly before he dies, Father Zossima preaches a sermon to his fellow monks in which he emphasizes the ungnostic nature of the gospel:

> My friends, pray to God for gladness. Be glad as children, as the birds of heaven. And let not the sin of men confound you in your doings. Fear not that it will wear away your work and hinder its being accomplished. Do not say: "Sin is mighty, wickedness is mighty, evil environment is mighty, and we are lonely and helpless. Evil environment is wearing us away and hindering our good work from being done." Fly from that dejection. There is only one means of salvation. Make yourself responsible for all men's sins. . . . Love to throw yourself on the earth and kiss it. Kiss the earth and love it with unceasing, consuming love. Love all men, love everything. Seek that rapture and ecstasy. Water the earth with the tears of your joy and love those tears.[9]

Father Zossima's vision is not a romantic or even a Franciscan exhortation to love "nature"; it is deeply incarnational. For in Christ, "all things in heaven and on earth were created, things visible and invisible . . . and in him all things hold together" (Col. 1:16–17). In him! This Word did not think time and place, Jewish flesh and history too contemptible a thing to assume. To make one's self responsible for all things is to acknowledge at the outset the scandalous earthiness of God's becoming flesh in Jesus Christ; it is to honor the indissoluble unity of God's life and all creation sealed in the flesh of this Word. The incarnation means that we are not permitted to loathe what God has loved. Indeed, God's coming to us in the flesh is what gives us the strength, Father Zossima thinks, to resist the "schismatic option"[10] that would put asunder what God has joined together in Christ. Gnostics seek to escape the misery and sin of a world they think unworthy of their love by opting for some cleaner, more spiritual or virtuous or rational realm above. To the extent that we seek to escape the world because we loathe its evil and sufferings, to the extent that we are contemptuous even of our own complicity in its misery and so yearn for a righteousness that will absolve us of any responsibility for this mess, to that extent we become schismatics ourselves, even terrorists of a sort who cultivate and live off the pride and resentment we harbor.

Gnostics, both ancient and modern, are not dumb people. Neither are they insensitive or lacking in virtue. Their sense of justice is often keener than that of the most devout of believers, and their faith in the explanatory power of ideas is often worthy of praise if not emulation. Yet the Gospels are often scandalously hard on "good people" (witness the Pharisees) and even more embarrassing, if not wounding, to intelligent, well-educated types. Ignorance may not be piety, as Calvin claimed, but neither is knowledge the same thing as discipleship. When intelligence or virtue reduces the divine mystery of human creatureliness to an explanation, it is not long before the recalcitrant have to be "reeducated" by the "virtuous" and "smart."

But not even the threat of totalitarian "explanations" fully accounts for the danger that Dostoyevsky perceives here. Such explanations, after all, contain an element of hope, however distorted. No, what concerns Dostoyevsky is the effect that such gnostic solutions have on our souls, giving us permission to remain perpetually aloof, like the righteous elder brother who persists in his resentment and ingratitude and is damned to a loneliness that perceives something of the world's injustice but none of its wonder and joy, much less his father's forgiving love. Gnostics are, Dostoyevsky thinks, joyless folk, whose particular hell is to be caught up in the virtue and comprehensiveness of their own explanations, oblivious to the grace that flows from God's embrace of this world in Jesus Christ.

In this sense, these gnostics are also, Charles Taylor writes, schismatics (in Russian, *raskolniki*) in the most profound sense of the word. They are

> cut off from the world and hence grace. They cannot but wreak destruction. The noblest wreak it only on themselves. The most base destroy others. Although powered by the noblest sense of the injustice of things, this schism is ulti-mately also the fruit of pride, Dostoyevsky holds. We sepa-rate because we don't want to see ourselves as part of the evil; we want to raise ourselves above it, away from the blame for it. . . . What will transform us is an ability to love the world and ourselves, to see it as good in spite of the wrong. But this will only come to us if we can accept being part of it, and that means accepting responsibility. Just as "no one is to blame" is the slogan of materialist revolutionaries, so "we are all to blame" is of Dostoyevsky's healing figures. Loving the world and ourselves is in a sense a miracle, in face of all the evil and degradation that it and we contain. But the miracle comes on us if we accept being part of it. . . . We become capable of love through being loved. . . . Dostoyevsky brings together here a central idea of the Christian tradition, especially evi-dent in the Gospel of John, that people are transformed through being loved by God.[11]

"We become capable of love through being loved." That is Dostoyevsky's great discovery and what he thinks the modern world has forgotten or is embarrassed to confess, preferring instead to justify itself unmiraculously in terms of this or that sec-ular or political or even religious "explanation." Such "theories," Dostoyevsky suspects, no matter how enlightened or progressive or virtuous—indeed the more enlightened, progressive, and vir-tuous they are, the more lethally destructive they will be—have the power to obscure from us the single greatest mystery of all, the mystery of God's goodness in the flesh, of God's love for sin-ners in Jesus Christ. That mystery is neither for the elite few nor for only those concerned with their own salvation, but is a miracle that reveals itself in its true dimensions as a mystery in the ordinary, creaturely, communal, limited, often humble and quite unspectacular flesh that Christ has assumed in his own body. There is where joy begins and where it is ever to be found. Dostoyevsky speaks of this miracle not by "spiritualizing" it and never by rendering it sentimental, but rather by depicting it in the form of a crisis that causes his characters to stumble, even fall upon its grace. When Father Zossima dies, for example, Alyosha is convinced that his mentor's saintliness will be manifest by the incorruptibility of the dead monk's remains. Here, he thinks, will be a sign of the saint's true spirituality: his bodily remains will be immune from earthly decay and become spiritualized, separated from the vagaries of mortal existence as a living relic of saintliness.

But that is not what happens. To the embarrassment of the faithful and the delight of the unbelievers, Father Zossima's body begins to stink. "His teaching was false," some declare; "he taught that life is a great joy and not a vale of tears."[12] Alyosha, on hearing this news, is crestfallen and turns to leave the monastery, not looking at his fellow monks as he walks away. "Have you, too, fallen into temptation?"[13] Father Paissy asks. Alyosha makes no answer but merely waves his hand and turns toward the gates of the monastery to leave.

What happens next is not a defining moment of faith or even some ecstatic religious experience but a temptation that comes to one whose faith has been shaken. Echoing the schismatic creed of his brother Ivan, Alyosha says, "I am not rebelling against my God. I simply 'don't accept his world.'"[14] Rakitin, a friend who is secretly pleased that Alyosha has stumbled, hopes to undermine the young monk's faith by proving that he is a dirty sinner like everyone else. He invites Alyosha to go with him to visit the beautiful young seductress Grushenka, hoping that she will draw Alyosha into her web and bring him down. She is in on this scheme and has paid Rakitin twenty-five rubles to bring Alyosha to her.

Grushenka has been the object of desire for both Alyosha's father, Fyodor, and his brother Dmitri. When Rakitin introduces Alyosha, she greets him teasingly and offers to sit on his lap: "I'll cheer you up, my pious boy," she says. "You'll let me sit on your knee, you won't be angry?"[15] Alyosha does not speak, but in listening to her talk he is surprised to discover that he senses no lust for her but only a kind of love that is struck by her humanity. When she is told that Alyosha's hero and mentor Father Zossima has died, Grushenka gets off his knee, crosses herself, and looks in sorrow at Alyosha. He then tells Rakitin, "I came here to find a wicked soul—I felt drawn to evil because I was base and evil myself, and I've found a true sister. She had pity on me just now. . . . Grushenka, I am speaking of you. You've raised my soul from the depths." Grushenka smiles at him and says, "Alyosha, your words make me feel ashamed, because I am bad and not good—that's what I am." And to Rakitin she says, "He called me his sister and I shall never forget that. Only let me tell you, Rakitin, though I am bad, I did give away an onion."[16]

Grushenka then tells Alyosha and Rakitin the parable of the onion. The story concerns a wicked peasant woman who has died and whose soul has been plunged into hell for her evil deeds. She has, however, a guardian angel who pleads with God on her behalf. God tells the angel that if he can find a single good deed that the woman performed, that deed would be enough to release her from hell. The angel finds that once this woman gave an onion to a beggar. Find that onion, God tells the angel, and it will be strong enough to pull her out of hell. The angel finds the onion and extends it to the woman in hell, who grabs its roots and slowly is pulled out of the lake of fire. The others who are doomed in hell, seeing the woman being lifted, grab her. She kicks them away, saying, "I'm to be pulled out, not you. It's my onion, not yours."[17] No sooner does she say that than the onion breaks and she falls back into hell.

Grushenka proceeds to confess her life to Alyosha, telling him things she has not told another, and finally says, "I've been waiting all my life for someone like you. I knew that someone like you would come and forgive me. I believed that, nasty as I am, someone would really love me, not only with a lustful love!" Alyosha takes her hand and replies, "I only gave you an onion, nothing but a little onion, that was all."[18]

"We learn to love as we are loved" might serve as the moral of this little vignette, but what is going on here is so much more than such a moral lesson. The temptation that confronts Alyosha is precisely that of separating body from soul, spirit from flesh. Grushenka's humanity is irreducible, he discovers, and evokes from Alyosha love for her as a child of God. Grushenka is not spiritualized into something she is not, nor are her failings overlooked. The end of the scene suggests, in fact, that this action of grace has had only a momentary effect on her. Still, she has come to know that she is loved, just as Alyosha in his grief has discovered grace in an unexpected place. Thinking to reject God's world, he finds in this rejected sinner a word of grace that ties him even more closely to its astonishing earthiness.

Finally and most importantly, the parable suggests that salvation is not an individual journey of self-discovery in which the gift of knowing God becomes a story about one's self. The salvation revealed in this parable is intensely social and has to do with other people. In this life and the next we travel in the company of saints, without whose help none of us can know God or ourselves. And the moment we think salvation is for us alone is the moment we enter hell.

From this temptation, Alyosha returns to the monastery. In a novel that is full of deeply moving scenes, the most moving of all unfolds as his call to ministry is confirmed in his joyful embrace of a messy, sinful, broken world.

Returning to the monastery late at night, Alyosha hears a monk reading John's Gospel over the dead and decaying body of Father Zossima. Father Paissy has come to the story of the wedding at Cana, and Alyosha hears him read, "And when they wanted wine, the mother of Jesus saith unto him, 'They have no wine.'" Alyosha thinks to himself:

Ah yes, I was missing that, and I didn't want to miss it, I love that passage: it's Cana of Galilee, the first miracle. . . . Ah, that miracle! Ah, that sweet miracle! It was not men's grief, but their joy Christ visited. He worked his first miracle to help men's gladness. . . . "He who loves men loves their gladness too. . . . There's no living without joy."

Father Paissy continues to read, and Alyosha imagines the wedding scene, where he sees, to his surprise, Father Zossima walking toward him, a "little, thin old man, with tiny wrinkles on his face, joyful and laughing softly." "Come and join us," Father Zossima tells him.

> We are rejoicing. . . . We are drinking the new wine, the wine of new, great gladness. . . . Why do you wonder at me? I gave an onion to a beggar, so I, too, am here . . . only one little onion. . . . What are all our deeds? And you, my gentle one, you, my bad boy, you too have known how to give a famished woman an onion today. Begin your work, dear one, begin it, gentle one! . . . Do you see our Son, do you see Him?

Alyosha replies that he is afraid to look, but Zossima encourages him.

> "Do not fear Him. He is terrible in his greatness, awful in His sublimity, but infinitely merciful. He has made Himself like unto us from love and rejoices with us. He is changing the water into wine that the gladness of the guests may not be cut short. He is expecting new guests. . . ." Something glowed in Alyosha's heart. . . . Tears of rapture rose from his soul. . . . He stretched out his hands, uttered a cry and waked up.[19]

Alyosha stops for a moment, looks at the coffin to make sure that his beloved mentor was in fact dead, and then "turned sharply and went out of the cell."

> He did not stop on the steps either, but went quickly down; his soul overflowing with rapture, yearned for freedom, space, openness. The vault of heaven, full of soft, shining stars, stretched vast and fathomless above him. The Milky Way ran in two pale streams from the zenith to the horizon. The fresh motionless, still night enfolded the earth. The

white towers and golden domes of the church gleamed out against the sapphire sky. The autumn flowers, in the garden, were slumbering. The silence of earth seemed to melt into the silence of the heavens. The mystery of earth was one with the mystery of the stars. . . . Alyosha stood, gazed out before him and then suddenly threw himself down on the earth. He did not know why he embraced it. He could not have told why he longed so irresistibly to kiss it, to kiss it. But he kissed it weeping and watering it with his tears, and vowed passionately to love it, to love it forever and ever. "Water the earth with the tears of your joy and love those tears." His elder's words echoed in his soul. . . . Within three days he left the monastery in accordance with the words of his elder, who had bidden him to "go forth into the world."[20]

"The silence of earth seemed to melt into the silence of the heavens. The mystery of earth was one with the mystery of the stars." Heaven and earth are inseparably united in this moment of rapturous joy, even as Alyosha throws himself on the earth to kiss it. This is the place God's love inhabits, where it is known, embraced, and celebrated. Despite the rapturous ecstasy of this novelistic vision, there could be no more powerful affirmation of the earthiness of God's love for this world and no greater clue that in this embrace of creation Dostoyevsky thinks we faithfully correspond to God's joyful embrace of this world.

A fictional visit to the home of a prostitute and a rapturous kissing of the earth might seem an odd way to picture the joy of ministry. These seem to be gestures at best, not an argument or program. Yet gestures, like prophetic signs, can speak volumes and reveal more than one might think, and more than many arguments or programs. So what conclusions about ministry can one draw from these gestures?

The rapturous embrace of the earth suggests that the joy of ministry is not to be found in theories about ministry or in the mastery of professional skills or even in the ethics or theology of ministry.

The joy of ministry is rooted in God's joyful embrace of this earth in Jesus Christ. The joy of ministry is a quite earthy joy. What else would one expect from the gospel of the incarnate God?

Moreover, the Holy Spirit, unlike other spirits, is not embarrassed by such earthiness or ashamed of uniting us to the body of Christ in baptism or nourishing us with Christ's body and blood, or giving us joy by calling us to serve in very particular places of ministry. In Christ's body we are united with others whom we have not chosen yet who become our mentors, friends, family, neighbors, brothers and sisters, common heirs to the grace of life. These folk are not inventions of our own or projects we undertake, nor are they "explanations" that will somehow liberate us from our earthly confines to another, purer realm. They are the simple, fleshly, and quite human gifts in the context of which we find our life and joy.

What obscures that joy and leaches out its delight is not just contempt for the humble or even ordinary nature of these gifts but also the suspicion that ministry is primarily a journey of self-discovery in which life in the Spirit is something to be kept well clear of life in the body. That is how faith is reduced to a "spirituality" that often recoils in the face of the messy ecclesial flesh, which is the body of Christ. It is a recurring temptation for American Protestants, especially, to want a nonecclesial relationship with God, to have a Jesus without his body. It is even more tempting for pastors to want this and, worse, to believe that their vocation is about their own journey, the congregation providing more or less pleasant background scenery for the pastor's ruminations or religious insights. As a result, many graduating seminarians find their first pastoral encounters with a congregation to be a rude awakening, even a kind of "rough wooing" in which an enormous amount of time is spent learning to "embrace the earth," that is, coming to a deeper understanding of the particular place this part of the body of Christ inhabits.

Alyosha's rapturous embrace of the earth suggests one further thought about the joy of ministry, and that has to do with theology and the worshiping community. Alyosha's gesture indicates a turning away from an ardently pursued "spiritual life" and a turning toward a life of ministry among the families and neighbors of his little town. By the end of the novel he is pastoring twelve schoolboys in whose lives he has brought healing and hope and with whom he reflects on the meaning of the resurrection after the death of one of their comrades. All this suggests that the joy of ministry is deeply related to the core narrative of the gospel itself and cannot emerge apart from the theological convictions and the community that narrative makes possible.

Gnosticism is a theological problem. As is boredom. And pride and contempt. Those who do not recognize the theological nature of ministry will only contribute to its joylessness, even if they fashion the most skilled practitioners of the art. Alyosha's discovery was a profoundly theological one about the nature of God and the world. His ministry throughout the rest of the novel is an embodied refutation of every explanation offered to justify religious or intellectual or moral self-centeredness. He becomes a witness, not because he knows everything or even because he knows himself, but because he knows God, the God who has made himself knowable in the person of Jesus Christ. That is not nothing. Indeed, that is the one thing that sustains him through failure after failure. The end of the novel deals explicitly with death, our final failure, and Alyosha bears witness to the simple joy of the Easter message. That is theology of the highest order.

And it takes place in the context of a community of faith, which is where theology is most at home. Seminaries and divinity schools have much to recommend them and have provided at their best a wonderful place to listen even more carefully and deliberately to the gospel's story, even forming ministers in their calling. But theologically they are one step removed from the place where theology has its true home, and to that extent they are more vulnerable to those explanations that seek to talk about God or even protect God from the idolatrous who would say too much. To be sure, the community gathered for worship is vulnerable to different or even worse explanations, but as David Johnson has noted, theology is finally "doxology: theology is worship. Words about God are words of praise."[21] Theology loses its joy to the extent that it loses contact with the language and the life of the worshiping community, that most ungnostic of things, a gathering of ordinary sinners around a table and font and pulpit, drawn into the gospel's story and being fed by it and offering their voices in gratitude and praise to the Word made flesh. What could be less spectacular, spiritually elite, or theoretical than that?

The last words of Johnson's article make clear the connection between the worshiping community, theology, and the joy of ministry.

> The lifeblood of theology is the worshipping community, and a theology that is done apart from the worshipping community is anemic, bloodless, pale and dead. Theology's home is not in the university or the seminary; theology's home is in the sanctuary. . . . "Glory to God in the highest," sang the angels; surely a good theology. "Glory to God in the highest." That is where theology begins. "Glory to God in the highest." That is where theology ends. And on earth? On earth there is a manger, and a baptism, and a calling, and miracles and healings, and oppositions and curses, and a farewell, and a betrayal, and a beating, and a cross, and a tomb. "Glory to God in the highest," sang the angels. But as St. Teresa of Avila was fond of remarking, "We're not angels." We here on earth sing "Glory to God in the highest" from the foot of the cross, from the mouth of the tomb. We sing in the midst of suffering and pain, of the evil we have done and the evil which has been done unto us, of a life which is indeed filled with the knowledge of both good and evil. "Glory to God in the highest." We sing in the night. But morning is promised, and is coming. "Glory to God in the highest." That is theology. That is life.[22]

And, one might add, that is joy.

Chapter Five

Practicing the Scales of Rejoicing

The Lord's Day and the Joyful Feast of the People of God

To-day, we find Good Friday easy to accept: what scandalises us is Easter: Modern man finds a happy ending, a final victory of Love over the Prince of this World, very hard to swallow.

—W. H. Auden[1]

In an early essay on Pushkin and Scriabin, of which only fragments remain, Mandelstam was evidently trying to find the source of this joy within the terms of Christianity. Christian art is joyous because it is free, and it is free because of the fact of Christ's having died to redeem the world. One need not die in art nor save the world in it, those matters having been, so to speak, attended to. What is left? The blissful responsibility to enjoy the world.

—Clarence Brown[2]

To be joyful in the worship of the living God is to be redeemed from all boredom.

—Arthur C. McGill[3]

I n her most comically redemptive story, Flannery O'Connor describes a Georgia farmwife standing in a field at dusk looking up at a bruised and swollen sky whose purple streak arcs downward, connecting heaven to earth. Ruby Turpin looks at this purple streak "as if she were absorbing some abysmal and life-giving knowledge." Ruby has been through a lot in this story, including sitting in a doctor's waiting room and being hit in the eye with a textbook on human development thrown at her by a young woman home from college. The wound has affected more than her eye, and the judgment it represents has caused Ruby to commit theology, that is, to question God's questioning of the neat and orderly arrangement she has constructed for her world. That is the abyss she is now looking into, the abyss of God's grace that has displaced her from the center of her own world and in doing so has provided her with "life-giving knowledge."

O'Connor's description of what Ruby sees is a vision of the kingdom of heaven.

> A visionary light settled in her eyes. She saw the streak as a vast swinging bridge extending upward from the earth through a field of living fire. Upon it a vast horde of souls were rumbling toward heaven. There were whole companies of white-trash, clean for the first time in their lives, and bands of black niggers in white robes, and battalions of freaks and lunatics shouting and clapping and leaping like frogs. And bringing up the end of the procession was a tribe of people whom she recognized at once as those who, like herself and Claud, had always had a little of everything and the God-given wit to use it right. She leaned forward to observe them closer. They were marching behind the others with great dignity, accountable as they had always been for good order and common sense and respectable behavior. They alone were on key. Yet she could see by their shocked and altered faces that even their virtues were being burned away.[4]

What makes this vision of the kingdom comically redemptive is not just the inclusion of all the "wrong people" but even more the liberation of the respectable folk from the terrible burden of their own virtues. That is what shocks and alters their faces.

Yet O'Connor's story does not end there. It is not simply a story of redemption's reordering of our loves, or even of the "abysmal" and "life-giving knowledge" that results from such a comic reversal.

For Ruby has been set free to hear and participate in the praise of God. Even though it is dark, she can now see the path that leads to her home. The last line of the story reads: "In the woods around her the invisible cricket choruses had struck up, but what she heard were the voices of the souls climbing upward into the starry field and shouting hallelujah."[5] The purging fires that have consumed her "virtues" have set her free to hear the praise of all creation and so to take up her rightful and happy place with other creatures in practicing the scales of rejoicing. The last note of this story is one of joy.

It would be too much to say that O'Connor's story is an invitation to faith, but it does possess some striking parallels to the liturgy of divine worship. There too we enter a sanctuary from which we expect a healing and redemptive word. There too we are struck by a word that does its work by altering our vision. It is a sharp word that wounds as it heals, dividing joint from marrow, "able to judge the thoughts and intentions of the heart" (Heb. 4:12). In its light we see the falseness that otherwise appears so sensible and right to us, and in its Word made flesh, we see what human development truly is. It is this Word that disrupts our world and liberates us from our virtues, compelling us to ask questions of the God we thought we knew but whose severe grace has revealed a vision of heaven that is at once both more manifold and more joyful than we ever expected. Like Dante, whose journey began "alone in a dark wood," we find ourselves in the end not alone, not simply with a new piece of self-knowledge, not simply wiser, but rather in the company of others looking away from ourselves to the "Eternal Fountain" before whose joy we are "lost in wonder, love, and praise."[6]

How does such joy happen? Or rather, how are we drawn into a chorus of praise that affords such marvelous self-forgetting? Must we too be struck by a book on human development?

Well, yes. That is why one worships. Or rather, that is why the worship of the God revealed in Jesus Christ so persistently intrudes on our schedules and sets us free for a life of joy and praise.

Karl Barth is one of the few theologians of the past century to have paid close attention to joy as an essential part of the Christian life. In his doctrine of creation, he speaks of the gift of joy in terms of our "freedom before God" and links its meaning to the commandment concerning the "Holy Day." Remembering the Sabbath Day to keep it holy has long been a characteristic emphasis of the Reformed faith. Still, this is not an obvious place to begin talking about human freedom or human joy. But Barth thinks how "the Holy Day" is kept reveals a great deal about what we think human beings are made for and to what end our days are put. The ethics of creation begin with this commandment because it "explains all the other commandments" by indicating that the "God who has created man and enabled and commissioned him to do his own work, is the God who is gracious to man in Jesus Christ."[7] As the particular celebration of the first day of the week, this commandment marks our freedom for God by turning us away from the tyranny of our own agendas and turning us toward what God has done in Jesus Christ, specifically the joyful Yes God has spoken in raising Jesus from the dead. This is the great, intrusive Easter particularity with which we have to deal. The particularity of this holy day shapes all our days and summons us to joy. We are to "hold to this Yes and not to anything else."[8]

Barth notices that the gospel "explains things" not by "explaining things" but by embodying itself in particular forms that begin to claim and shape our lives. Accordingly, knowledge of God becomes not a matter of intellectual assent to something we have decided is true, but the way God draws us into the particular shape of his body in the world. To overlook the particularity of the gospel is to miss the startling intimacy of the God who has come near to us in Jesus Christ. To be sure, "the Holy Day" forbids us to trust in our own work and calls us to acknowledge that all of our days belong to the One who has redeemed them all, but it does so not by committing us to some ethical ideal but by summoning us to the practice that honors a particular seventh of our days in the name of him who was raised on the first day of the week.

This particularity is part of the strangeness of the gospel. After all, the world functions just fine without noting that one day is different from any other day. Working 24/7 is thought by many to be an appropriate, even praiseworthy way of dealing with the world's serious matters. But just as the church lives out its special history of God's covenantal grace amid the more general and quite visible history of the world, and just as the church, in so doing, reveals the goal of that visible history to be hidden in God's providential love, so the particularity of the "the Holy Day" is a sign of contradiction against the world's idolatrous seriousness. Such seriousness can only be maintained by presuming that the gospel's story is about us, that at its center is our religious selves, and that our days are our own to use or spend as we see fit. Of course, such idolatry is lethal and like our hard-won virtues is in need of being exposed to the refining fires of God's comedic rest. The strange thing about the God of Jesus Christ is that this God can not only work, but this God can also rest from work, can have fellowship with others. Indeed, this God wills not to be known apart from the joyful sign of this fellowship, a sign of contradiction that mocks our otherwise busy schedules and desperate entertainments. This God is able to give sleep to his beloved (Ps. 127).[9]

Barth is aware that modernity is suspicious of such particularities, but he thinks that joy is inherently particular. "The Holy Day" offends in this regard, not just because its rest distinguishes the first day of the week from other days as the day of the resurrected Lord, but also because it dares to speak of the last day, the end and purpose of all of time.[10] End and purpose language offends against the modern illusion of limitless days, which have no particular end or purpose beyond what we give to them. Indeed, it is the central role of self in assigning meaning to our days that enables modernity to "deny death" [11] so casually and be so eager to shoulder the intolerable burdens of self-justification. Here too, however, it is "through the cross that joy comes into the world." For it is through the cross that the illusion of our "deathlessness" itself dies and our life is revealed as being "hidden with Christ in God" (Col. 3:3). The joy of his Easter victory is the joy of God's laughter overcoming death's dreadful seriousness, revealing Christ to be our life (Col. 3:4) and setting the terms by which the joy of his Sabbath will interrupt succeeding centuries with the weekly gift of worship.

That is how the particularity of the Sabbath "de-centers" us, Barth thinks, from the worlds and agendas we construct and reorients us toward reality, that is, toward God. In this sense, keeping the Sabbath in an all-too-serious world is a way of affirming our freedom, of embracing the comedic truth about the God who saves by grace and has made us to glorify and enjoy him. Of course, we are not able to do this on our own. It is the regular intrusion of God's gracious Sabbath on "our time" that summons us to receive time as God's gracious gift, teaching us so to number our days, that the boring seriousness of our agendas might be displaced by a wisdom that can rejoice and rest and even play. Sunday is meant for joy.[12]

In a way that might seem surprising in one who wrote thirteen volumes of *Church Dogmatics*, Barth seems curiously unimpressed with the seriousness of his own labors. The joy of "Sunday freedom" has implications also for the theologian. In one of his essays on Shakespeare, W. H. Auden praises him for not trying to write "great drama." "There's something a little irritating," Auden writes, "in the determination of the very greatest artists, like Dante, Joyce, Milton, to create masterpieces and to think themselves important. To be able to devote one's life to art without forgetting that art is frivolous is a tremendous achievement of personal character. Shakespeare never takes himself too seriously."[13] Nor, might one add, did Mozart.

Barth hardly thought theology frivolous, but in many ways it was his great achievement not to ask theology to do more than it could properly do. One of the reasons *Church Dogmatics* is so massive is that it is so exuberant, so full of joyful confidence in what God has done and is doing and will do, and so enraptured with retracing the lineaments of God's grace. Accordingly, Barth can listen carefully to Scripture's story and the church's reflection on that story and rejoice not in merely repeating the same words but in trying to say the same thing in other words, even in more faithful words, in words that bear witness to the gospel in one's own time and place. Such a task is itself a form of discipleship, an obedient "following after" that leads not to a sacrifice of the intellect but to its flourishing, even to more daring turns of thought and richer depictions of faithfulness. Such theological joy has nothing to do with trying to prove something. Rather, it sings. It is natural theology, on the other hand, that is unmusical. True theology is always doxology and is able to laugh even at its own efforts. Barth writes:

> The angels laugh at old Karl. They laugh at him because he tries to grasp the truth about God in a book of Dogmatics. They laugh at the fact that volume follows volume and each is thicker than the previous one. As they laugh, they say to one another, "Look! Here he comes with his little pushcart full of volumes of the Dogmatics!" And they laugh about the men who write so much about Karl Barth instead of writing about the things he is trying to write about. Truly the angels laugh.[14]

Theology too, theology especially, is rooted in the gift of Sabbath joy. Or better, Sabbath joy holds special blessing for the theologian and pastor, whose task is to tell and retell the story of the crucified and risen Lord. As such, theology can never be a heavy labor. For since the Easter victory is true, since Jesus really does live and reign, theology is set free to be grateful, to praise, even to play. Bearing witness to God's grace, Barth writes, is no trivial matter, "but in its freedom from purpose it has more of the nature of a game or song than of work or warfare."[15] In an ad hominem remark to pastors who are sometimes tempted to take themselves very seriously, he writes:

> As we all know the minister's Sunday involves both a program and a work, yet does this mean that he has to bemoan it? Is not the minister the ideal case of the man who works joyfully on the holy day and in this very way keeps it holy? If it were toilsome and dull for ministers to do their Sunday work, how could they expect the congregation and the world to find it refreshing? More generally, we may ask whether even during the week theology is a *labor operosus*, a burden and anxiety, something which has to be done for professional reasons but which we should not be happy to lay aside with a clear conscience. *If theology as such is not a joy to the theologian, if in his theological work he is not genuinely free from care, what is it?* Can he abandon it on Sunday and devote himself

to all sorts of tomfoolery? Why should he not be free for theology? . . . Fundamentally, cannot the heaviest theological
working day be for him the best day of rest?[16]

The "infallible criterion of Sabbath observance," according to
Barth, is "whether and how sincerely we are in a position to celebrate it as a true day of joy."[17] Idolatry is always very serious. Sunday freedom is able to rejoice. It is a feast that is characterized by
its "release from care" and "lack of programme," by freedom from
the "harsh seriousness" and "self-justification" that requires either
entertainment or dutiful labor to distract it from itself.

The gospel's story, Barth thinks, is not dull. Why should worship be? The gospel's message is not about "the devil or capitalism or communism or human folly and wickedness in general" but
about the lordship of Jesus Christ. His "clear and unambiguous
Yes" to us is, for all its grace, quite sharp enough to judge, attack,
and be critical of the idols to which we are tempted to give our
worship, both those sentimental ones that lie about the cross and
those sadder ones that refuse the joy of the resurrection.[18] But the
day is to be a day of joy because it is the day of God's Yes.

Moreover, this Yes of God is not a private word or intellectual
construct but a word that creates community. The joy it makes
possible is a shared gift in which we are able to enter the fellowship of "service and prayer and not least of song."[19] "Come,
rejoice with me" is the constant refrain of Jesus' parables (Luke
15). The joy of the day is, in large measure, expressing with others delight and gratitude to God who has created us to share in
such joy. The triune God is not wrapped in solitary loneliness but
lives in the joy of that self-giving and receiving that is Father, Son,
and Holy Spirit. How can the Lord's Day not also be a day that
celebrates life together?

And just so, it can never be a day of mere renunciation or silence.
What marks this day of joy off from the idolatries of self is that
God's Yes does not silence those who hear it in awe-struck terror
but evokes their praise, enabling them to sing, to rejoice, to
become articulate in the knowledge of God and themselves. We
learn to speak the joy of God by having it spoken to us. And this

joy becomes our praise precisely as we acknowledge and echo it forth. For Barth, there is a sense in which we do not know what we know until we can voice what we know, or better, we do not know what joy is until we sing and speak it.[20] Later, in speaking about prayer, Barth notes that we pray not out of some inner need but "because God who has spoken to man expects man in return to speak with Him."[21] God has made us to be a conversation partner, and his Yes to us graciously enables us to respond in joy. Joy is most often a voiced gift, something that is sung, sounded forth, even laughed in its praise.

What does it mean, then, to praise God? It means to rejoice not only in God's mighty acts but also and particularly to rejoice that God's mighty acts include our being God's articulate creatures who may know and love God and offer ourselves to him.

> The fact that the work of the mouth alone is not enough, that there is mere lip confession resting on no true knowledge and therefore empty, does not alter in the slightest the fact that the confession to God which is concretely demanded is also a confession of the lips. It is in his spoken word that man, like God, comes out into the open, making himself clear, intelligible and in some way responsible, venturing forth and binding and committing himself. In his word man hazards himself . . . coming out into the open as a partisan of God.[22]

The joy of ministry is not unrelated to this "coming out into the open as a partisan of God." Openly rejoicing in the goodness of God's grace, even dancing as David did before the ark of the covenant, will always occasion a certain bafflement and even scorn among the more responsible and serious men and women of the world, but there is something quite irresponsible about the gospel's good news. And one cannot know the joy of ministry "without the risk of being ludicrous." Indeed, a follower of Jesus Christ "is one who is not ashamed to do something quite useless in a world of serious purposes."[23]

It is not surprising that the three practices that Barth lifts up as joyfully obedient ways of responding to God's Yes to us in Jesus

Christ are all, from one point of view, quite impractical. Keeping the Sabbath, risking open identification as a follower of Jesus Christ, and praying seem odd ways of claiming our freedom as God's human creatures and even odder ways of transforming the world. Such practices do not "do" anything. They are not efficient. They compel us to cease from our work, to sing or even dance, and to speak to God. As we have already seen, these practices "decenter" us from our world, which in itself is both an unmodern and even more unpostmodern thing to do. In commenting on the last question of the Heidelberg Catechism ("What is the meaning of the little word 'Amen'?"), Barth notes how this catechism's answer ("Amen means, this shall be true and certain. For my prayer is much more certainly heard by God than I feel in my heart that I desire such from Him.") "is still uninfected by Cartesianism. It is not as if our prayer were the certain thing and [God's] hearing the uncertain, but precisely the opposite. We can doubt the value, power, and sincerity of our own asking, but not God's hearing. . . . It is because it is heard that we pray, and not because we are so skilled in the asking."[24]

What decenters us, what proves so inefficient and useless in a world bent on taking itself seriously, most especially its religious self, is the eternally rich God whose joy subverts our efforts and reorients us to reality. Celebrating the Sabbath, confessing Christ, and praying are not exercises in piety that will inevitably produce good pastors and teachers; much less are they forms of self-expression that grow out of our own need. They are the not-to-be-despised tools God gives us for "practicing the scales of rejoicing,"[25] enabling us to claim our freedom as human creatures who are made for doxology. It is in the praise of God that our humanity flourishes, and as we find joy there we discover it in the other strange places God has put it in the world: in the least of these, in the lilies of the field, even in the cross whose radical decentering of every sinner brings joy into the world.

⚜⚜⚜⚜⚜

It seems appropriate to bring this chapter to a close by reflecting with Barth on how joy as he has described it is related to the cross of Jesus Christ. Barth begins this discussion with a lengthy meditation on the theological significance of illness and death. In noting the healing miracles of Jesus and his rejection of illness as a distortion of God's good creation, Barth recalls the work of the nineteenth-century evangelist and healer Johann Christoph Blumhardt (1805–80) and his indignation at the way illness, disease, and death contradict the gospel's claims. "Jesus is Victor!" Blumhardt famously proclaimed, indicating his belief that what happened in Jesus signifies God's utter triumph over death and its threats to bring creation to nothing.

> Blumhardt realized, in contrast to all older Protestantism and basically to the whole of Western Christendom, that in this name [of Jesus] not just a psychic but a historical and even cosmic decision is made, and a question not only of disposition but of power is raised. . . . Blumhardt missed even in the Jesus of contemporary Pietists the repugnance of the real Jesus at the grave of Lazarus and His will to help and fight and reign. Blumhardt took up the struggle because he was bound and liberated by this royal repugnance of Jesus. . . . Hence the famous words with which he opened the contest in the case of Gottliebin [Dittus, a young woman suffering from a nervous disorder]: "Fold your hands and pray: Lord Jesus, help me! We have seen long enough what the devil does; now we shall see what the Lord Jesus can do." Hence his statement in his later account of the matter: "I was ashamed before myself and my Savior . . . to give into the devil. I often had to ask myself, Who is the Lord?, and, trusting Him who is the Lord, I always heard the inward call to advance."[26]

Barth does not think Blumhardt another Mary Baker Eddy any more than he thinks the gospel is a form of Christian Science. He knows that disease and death cannot be removed by our exertions, no matter how pious or faithful, and that in God's providence, disease and even death can sometimes be welcome. Still, if Jesus is Victor over disease and death, his faithfulness enables such suffering to be patiently borne and to be received in the confidence that though disease and death might well triumph over our lives, they have no place in God's kingdom and cannot do what they seek to do, that is, frustrate God's purpose or separate us from God's love. For that reason, one can even talk about joy in the midst of suffering, perhaps even begin to talk about joy precisely there.

Toward the end of his life, Barth himself was quite sick, and at one time in 1965 he was hospitalized for four months. In a letter to a friend, Barth wrote, not entirely tongue in cheek:

> Somewhere within me there lives a bacillus with the name *proteus mirabilis*, which has an inclination to enter my kidneys—which would then mean my finish. I am certain that this monstrosity does not belong to God's good creation, but rather has come in as a result of the Fall. It has in common with sin and with the demons also that it cannot simply be done away with but can be only despised, combated, and suppressed. . . . But the main thing is the knowledge that God makes no mistakes and the *proteus mirabilis* has no chance against him.[27]

Joy, Barth thinks, really is at the heart of the gospel's message. He notes how much attention Scripture gives to "delight, joy, bliss, exultation, merry-making and rejoicing."[28] Moreover, he does not think that the gloom of God's judgment on Israel or the call to penitence with which John the Baptist introduces the New Testament or even the terrible darkness of the crucifixion itself signify

> a suppression of the joy to which there is constant reference . . . , but it seems rather as if this joy and summons arise from these dark places, and that what is declared from this center is glad tidings. Why? Because God the Creator and Lord of life acts and speaks here, taking the lost cause of man out of his hand and making it His own, intervening majestically, mercifully, and wisely for him. Now obviously what arises at this dark source is not a random or arbitrary joy. It is not unqualified, but supremely qualified. What is here

regarded as joy, and is this, has obviously passed through a catalysator. It has been destroyed on the one hand and reconstituted on the other. But it has been reconstituted and validated, and even raised to the level of a command. Christ is risen; He is truly risen. Joy is now joy before the Lord and in Him. It is joy in His salvation, His grace, His law, His whole action. But it is now genuine, earthly, human joy: the joy of harvest, wedding, festival, and victory; . . . the joy in which one may and must drink wine as well as eat bread, sing and play as well as speak, dance as well as pray. We must not forget the catalysator [the cross] without which it cannot be the obedient joy demanded. But we must also remember that the man who hears and takes to heart the biblical message is not only not permitted but plainly forbidden to be anything but merry and cheerful.[29]

"The luxury of false religion," wrote Sydney Smith, "is to be unhappy."[30] The point of Barth's exegesis is not that faith is required to be "up" all the time, much less suffused with optimism, but that the grace of God liberates us to be thankful. That is what it means to be truly free. Joy is nothing more than "the simplest form of gratitude."[31]

The joy of the gospel distinguishes itself from its idolatrous counterfeits in its explicit confession that life, in both its miseries and its moments of happiness, is a gift from God, whose goodness cannot simply be dismissed or ignored. Though joy can hardly be manufactured and is in its most basic form anticipatory, the Christian is called to be ready to rejoice, "not merely to hurry on with his own work, but pause in gratitude for what life really is as the gift of God." As the Sabbath interrupts the working week to enable us to receive all our days as a gift, so does this faithful "readiness for joy" enable us to discover God's presence in the unlikeliest of places, even "to look out for opportunities for gratitude."[32]

Barth is aware that to talk like this runs the risk of being accused of "willing joy," as if this were another way of manipulating God's grace to our favor. He writes:

In true joy there can never lack great or small enterprises to make it possible, to prepare and accomplish it. And it is in this inward and indeed, outward preparation that joy is usually experienced most intensively as the joy of anticipation. But we must consider carefully that real joy comes and is present like the Holy Spirit. Indeed, it is really when the Holy Spirit comes and is present that one experiences true joy. But this means that joy comes and is present as it lists, and no one knows whence it comes or whither it goes. We can create opportunities for it in anticipatory joy, but we cannot create or construct or produce or force it by various plans and measures.[33]

One such opportunity is worship. And like worship, joy, Barth thinks, is known where and when the Spirit gathers the community to receive the shared gift of life together in Jesus Christ. "There may be cases where a man can be really merry in isolation. But these are exceptional and dangerous. . . . It certainly gives us ground to suspect the nature of his joy as real joy if he does not desire—'Rejoice with me'—that at least one or some or many others . . . should share this joy."[34]

Moreover, joy is not quantifiable. Indeed, the great joy of the Easter message is what invites us to rejoice in the small joys of God's Easter people. Joy is never compulsive, Barth thinks, but comes most often in simple things: our cohumanity, friendship, nature, or even in work. Work can provide deep joy, especially the work of the minister, who can only fail to find joy in pastoral work by willfully ignoring and even dishonoring the nature of this calling. That is not to say ministry is always fun or even joyful. Many times it plunges one into misery, heartbreak, and defeat. Yet the joy of ministry is not offended at such things and, as Barth points out, even emerges from "dark places" as the singing of hymns arose from the Philippian jail.

Joy is most often not the euphoria of great success but a song that refuses to die on our lips, indeed, that carries us through the dark places to the light. That is why Dietrich Bonhoeffer taught his students at Finkenwalde to sing the spirituals he had learned in Harlem while studying at Union Seminary in New York (and perhaps also why these spirituals were sung in the first place), and why even while imprisoned during the terror of a bombing raid, he could write of the joy of hearing a chorale ("What God does is well done") as "a good beginning to the day."[35]

What is one to make of such joy? That Bonhoeffer, like Mother Teresa or Dr. Martin Luther King Jr., is such a heroic example that we are only confirmed in the smallness of our own faith? That lacking the drama of a Nazi prison or the misery of the streets of Calcutta or the lunging police dogs of Birmingham, we grow perversely nostalgic for such clearly drawn evils (that we know little about), ashamed of our poor efforts to sing the Lord's song in less threatening settings? Must one "rush to the barricades" to experience joy? And what is to keep joy in our day from being confused with entertainment or that kind of happiness that an entertainment culture fosters in such abundance, yet another commodity to distract us from other distractions? Can we ever truly know what joy is?

Barth reminds us that joy, first of all, belongs to God and not to us. It is an attribute of God's glory, a gift of God's triune life, which means that only God can make joy known and knowable, and like all of God's gifts, the gift of joy can only be defined in terms of God's self-giving. The clue to God's self-giving is Jesus Christ, who was no stranger to suffering or want. In the end, his whole life came under the shadow of the cross. If joy is to be found, it must be found there or not at all.

> We must not be surprised and angry that we live in this shadow. . . . We must also realize that all the provisional light which we believe we can recognize and enjoy as such really breaks forth from this shadow, that all the little fulfillments in which we may rejoice are only reflections of the great fulfillment which has taken place in the darkness into which God Himself entered for us in His Son, and that every recognition and experience of these fulfillments is only an advance towards the comprehensive and conclusive revelation of this great fulfillment. But this means in practice that the real test of our joy of life as commanded and therefore a true and good

joy is that we do not evade the shadow of the cross of Jesus Christ and are not unwilling to be joyful even as we bear the sorrows laid upon us. What if the true, the strongest, the most refreshing and enduring temporal fulfillments await us at the very point where in our simplicity, which might well be our blindness, we will not seek them, in the repulses, obstructions, and disturbances we meet, in our confrontation with the dark aspect of life, and even more so, in our confrontation with the death that has come into the world through sin.[36]

Joy is a christological category. To that extent, whatever we mean by joy has to come to terms with the Gospels' narrative of Jesus as the Joyful One. To say this risks turning Jesus into a "happy face," and that, of course, would be a deep betrayal of the gospel message. Yet the Gospels, as Alyosha Karamazov discovered, are not silent about Jesus' willingness to celebrate with others, even to bear with accusations of being a drunk and a glutton (Luke 7:34) or spoiling the almighty seriousness of the Pharisees' pursuit of righteousness. But the Gospels are even clearer that Jesus' path was, from the beginning, a path that led to the cross. Can joy be defined in terms of the cross?

The Stoics found solace in apathy, resignation, and self-control. But these virtues do not describe the Jesus who, as Hebrews 12:2 reminds us, endured the cross "for the sake of the joy that was set before him."

The joy of Jesus Christ is not a shallow thing or a monument to human self-control. Jesus, as every memorizer of Bible verses knows, wept. Yet such joy is able to encompass sorrow and proves itself in us, Barth maintains, "in the fact that our capacity for joy shows itself to be also a capacity for suffering, a readiness to accept with reverence and gratitude . . . the mystery and wonder of the life given to us by God . . . even where [this gift] presents itself to us in its alien form."[37]

The joy that knows suffering is the joy that is able to hope. And it is able to hope because the joy we know as disciples is anticipatory of the great joy that is to come. Joy's exuberance directs us toward heaven and is unafraid to speak of "the things that are above, where Christ is" (Col. 3:1). Yet this anticipation does not belittle or subvert the joys we know in the present, even when they seem small and unremarkable. Rather, our future hope only confirms the joys that we share in this life and compels us to embrace the beauty we see and the goodness we receive in all their earthly particularity and even brokenness. One need not be a Panglossian optimist to speak of the joy of the cross, the joy that is unashamed to love this sinful world so extravagantly. For the cross is not the way God covers up a bad job or becomes tragically resigned to the follies of his sinful children. The cross discloses the depths of God's joyful embrace of this world, revealing not only our sinful and broken and proud rejection of his love, but even more God's unwillingness to abandon us to our self-contrived kingdoms of misery. He takes our place and in the end will not even let us have our own misery to ourselves, no matter how hard won and deserving we think it may be.

There is something quite untragic about this comedy of redemption, almost as if God's grace triumphs by giving us joy, by refusing to let us cling to our own sullenness. That is the great temptation of "elder brothers" everywhere, and it is the gift of the gospel that the "waiting father" refuses to let them starve themselves on the sufficiency of their own virtues but invites them instead to celebrate and rejoice with others, to share in the laughter that exposes us all as sinners even as it enfolds in its forgiving arms.

In an essay on Elizabethan drama, W. H. Auden notes how different comedy is in a world that has heard the gospel and knows its story from the classical world of pagan antiquity. Classical comedy depends for its effects, he writes, "upon the division of mankind into two classes, those who have arête [virtue] and those who do not, and only the second class, fools, shameless rascals, slaves, are fit subject for comedy."

"But," he adds, "Christian comedy is based upon the belief that all men are sinners; no one, therefore, whatever his rank or talents can claim immunity from the comic exposure and, indeed, the more virtuous, in the Greek sense, a man is, the more he realizes that he deserves to be exposed." (This is why Ruby Turpin is such a comic figure.) In classical comedy, the rascals get what they deserve. In Christian comedy grace triumphs in forgiveness. "In classical comedy . . . when the curtain falls, the audience is laughing and those on stage are in tears. In Christian comedy . . . when the curtain falls, the audience and the characters are laughing together."[38] Which is perhaps not a bad description of that heavenly city whose joy all our joys anticipate, where, when the final curtain does come down, God will be with his people and "will wipe every tear from their eyes. Death will be no more; mourning and crying and pain will be no more, for the first things have passed away" (Rev. 21:4).

Chapter Six

The Splendid Embarrassment
Theology's Home and the Practice of Ministry

But it may be that it is not only *I* who say that our embarrassment is our promise. It may be that the living Truth beyond Yes and No, the reality of the living God beyond my dialectic turns, has of its own might and love ordained that promise should enter into our embarrassment. It may be that the Word, the word of God, which we ourselves shall never speak, has put on our weakness and unprofitableness so that *our* word *in* its very weakness and unprofitableness has become capable at least of being the mortal frame, the earthen vessel, of the word of God. It may be so, I say; and if it were, we should have reason not so much to speak of our need as to declare and publish the hope and hidden glory of our calling.

—Karl Barth[1]

The physical presence of other Christians is a source of incomparable joy and strength to the believer. . . . The believer feels no shame, as though he were still living too much in the flesh, when he yearns for the physical presence of other Christians. Man was created a body, the Son of God appeared on earth in the body, he was raised in the body, in the sacrament the believer receives the Lord Christ in the body, and the resurrection of the dead will bring about the perfected fellowship of God's spiritual-physical creatures. The believer therefore lauds the Creator, the Redeemer,

83

God, Father, Son and Holy Spirit, for the bodily presence of
a brother.
—Dietrich Bonhoeffer[2]

What is real piety? What is true attachment to the Church?
How are these fine feelings best evinced? The answer is
plain: by sending strawberries to a clergyman. Many thanks.
—Sydney Smith, to a parishioner[3]

One of the consequences of the fall, Charles Williams has suggested, is the suspicion surrounding the phrase "the joy of
obedience." This seemingly oxymoronic joining of terms tends to
baffle a culture that thinks the pursuit of happiness is a self-evident
good, a right, which must always bristle at any external claim on its
obedience. In his book *The Forgiveness of Sins*, Williams argues that
the right ordering of our salvation accomplished in Christ is the
right ordering of our life within "the body." To see the effect of sin
in our world, Williams proposes that we reverse the terms of Eph-
esians 4:15–16 ("But speaking the truth in love, we must grow up
in every way into him who is the head, into Christ, from whom the
whole body, joined and knit together . . .") to read, ". . . that we
may grow away from him in all things . . . the whole body disjoined
and decompacted."[4] The body splits, breaks apart, the knee bone
no longer connected to the thighbone, until all that is left is a val-
ley of dry bones, with each bone bleached and alone in splendid
isolation, a description, Williams thinks, of much of the way modern culture (and the contemporary church) feels.

What Williams sees very clearly is the corporal or communal
nature of redemption and the "spiritual" or otherwise disembodied nature of damnation, or what is sometimes called freedom. He
also sees that the forgiveness of sins in the person of Jesus Christ
is a healing accomplished by his "joyful obedience." Only in a fallen
world are obedience and joy split apart, just as service to Another
in that world must seem implausible as "perfect freedom." The
effect of sin is schismatic in this regard also, tearing apart things
that belong together. Williams notes, for example, how the word
"chastity" has for us mostly negative connotations, indicating some

form of heroic self-restraint or even quest for purity. But, in fact, chastity is "the obedience to and the relation with the adorable central body," the "glory" even of that divine Word in whom "all things hold together" (Col. 1:17). In this respect, chastity and courtesy are twins, the one being the love of the soul for God and the other the love of the soul for its created companions. Only our fallenness makes chastity an achievement and courtesy a matter of etiquette. Williams can even say that "chastity is courtesy towards God; courtesy is chastity toward men."[5]

Can ministry really take the form of joyful obedience? No one who has practiced ministry for long can maintain that it is glamorous work. The depiction of congregations "without spot or wrinkle" is rightly called "ecclesiastical pornography" by Eugene Peterson, who knows that pastors themselves are tempted to pose as centerfolds of successful churches.[6] Peterson notes that Scripture itself does not glamorize Israel, whose history is characterized less by success than by defeat and heartbreak, faithlessness and loss. He continues:

> A bare sixty or seventy years after Pentecost we have an account of seven churches that shows about the same quality of holiness and depth of virtue found in any ordinary parish in America today. In two thousand years of practice we haven't gotten any better. You would think we would have, but we haven't. Every time we open up a church door and take a careful, scrutinizing look inside we find them there again—sinners. Also Christ. Christ in the preaching, Christ in the sacraments, but inconveniently and embarrassingly mixed into this congregation of sinners.[7]

We find this mixture embarrassing because in a fallen world we too have become schismatics, tearing the grace of Christ apart from Christ's own body. We do this in a number of ways, the most obvious one being to spiritualize the faith and make it a journey of self-discovery. This is an old gnostic trick, but it never seems to wear itself out, and it has the advantage of protecting us from the gospel's embarrassing fleshliness while reassuring us that we are spiritually intact. Indeed, that is why most people go to seminary, William Willimon suspects—to become more "spiritual" or more "Christian." That is the only way, they think, that joy and obedience can be held together. Accordingly, training for ministry must become an individual if not private matter of spiritual growth and self-discovery. As a result, actual encounters with the church inevitably become rude awakenings whose dispiriting shocks and disappointing failures steadily undermine any joy in ministry. Ecclesial realities can be harsh, Willimon notes.

> You see, I'm not a "community person" by natural inclination. Tell me I have some charismatic flair for leadership. Praise me for the art of my preaching or the empathy of my pastoral care, just let me share myself and pour out my feelings, urge me to become a spiritual virtuoso, but please do not yoke me to the Body, do not marry me to that unruly Bride, do not force me to find what I do and therefore who I am among those who gather at my so very mundane congregation.
>
> Let me do freelance ministry, give me a degree and tell me I'm special, encourage me to tack up a shingle, allow me to have some exotic spiritual *gnosis* that makes me holy, but do not hold me accountable to the church. I love Jesus, and I want to serve Him. But He married beneath His station. For me the real scandal of ministry, the ultimate stumbling block, the thing I avoid and fear the most, is the church. Like many of you, I set out to serve God and ended up caught among those whom God served. My problem, my difficulty with the Spirit, is that it wants to tie me to the church.[8]

That is the strange thing about the Holy Spirit and what distinguishes it from other spirits: the Holy Spirit gathers dry bones to create a musculoskeletal form and, having covered the body with flesh and given it voice, enables the body to offer articulate praise. The image may well be from Ezekiel's vision, but it also has deep resonance with the resurrection narratives that depict Jesus as being raised from the dead in bodily form by the power of the

Holy Spirit, who is able also to give life to the scattered and often broken bones of the church's mortal body (Rom. 8:11). To walk by the Spirit is to inhabit this animated body, something that does not come naturally to any of us. Willimon is right to notice the awkwardness of ministry that is so tied to the body, but such awkwardness is itself a sign of its being a gift and not a possession. It is also a clue to the way joyful obedience begins to take shape.

For if ministry is best thought of as inescapably connected to the body, then its joys will always be the embodied ones that nourish life and celebrate its flourishing. Such joys will be the joys of the font, of being baptized into the body of Christ and discerning our true location in him, indeed, finding the place where we truly are who we are. Such joys will also be the joys of the table, of eating with others the food that sustains life and ministry in Christ and sharing with them the table fellowship of life together. But the joys of the table will be complemented by the joys of the Word, of the story that we are also invited to eat, the story that makes sense of all our eating and drinking. This Word brings with it also the joys of listening—a rare gift in our time—and study, and finally, the joys also of speaking, of daring to proclaim this Word from the pulpit, a Word that has gathered and sustained the community before the community was even a community. Often these joys will be the joys of conviviality, of listening and speaking, of inhabiting a particular place with known and unknown mysteries. But such joys will also be marked by the sharing of history and even suffering, the joys of not having and bearing with, of forgiving, and of living with parts of the story that are painful to hear.

Such joys are neither glamorous nor all that marketable in a consumer culture. They take time. They require collaboration. They are difficult to program. They are often quiet, though not always. More often they are hidden. Like seed that has fallen into the ground, such joys cannot always be seen at work. Still, it is not quite accurate to say, as Willimon implies, that we are simply "stuck" with them or with this awkward contraption called "the body of Christ." The church's life is not a concession to our weakness, much less an onerous burden every Christian is called to bear. Contradicting the barrenness of much of its life, and to its regular and utter astonishment, the church persistently *discovers* joy, its body possessing a splendor that is, despite our best efforts, inextinguishable.

We Protestants have long criticized any "theology of glory" that would make of the church an idol, but we have been less clear about the splendor of the church as that fellowship that participates in the life together of the triune God through the banquet Christ makes possible in his own body. Surely, this is where thinking about the practice of ministry should begin: with the joyful feast of the people of God, who feast on the obedience of Christ. He overcomes all our schismatic loves and divisions in his own body through the cross. In him we are located; in his body we are given the company of others; at his word ministry becomes not so much a project or a career as the risking of a joyful obedience that recklessly dares to follow him.

That is where all discipleship begins: with Christ's joyful obedience that has bound a world to God's own life and made a place for that life to be known and enjoyed and shared. Because he was joyfully obedient, the phrase cannot be oxymoronic or merely ironic but strangely, mysteriously, wonderfully true. And it must be true not in a rhetorical or sentimental or even liturgical sense, but true christologically, that is, as a joyful obedience that works itself out amid the hard realities of suffering, rejection, the cross, death, and hell. All of these and more threaten to separate us from the love of God, to make it possible for us to be truly schismatic, to think that we might indeed belong only to ourselves and to whatever sad joys we might devise. Schismatics are ever ready to be tragic figures. But Christ's joyful obedience will have none of that. His body continues to liberate us from the heavy burden of our grim self-centeredness. It is the happy task of the ministry of the church to proclaim, in the midst of such hard realities, that "we are not our own,"[9] and never have been, but that we belong to Christ, who has made a place for us within his own body precisely in the midst of such hard realities. In just this way, his joy becomes true also for us. Ministry in the church begins here, in the joy of these hard places, and cannot be found anywhere else.

Bodies, however, are extended in space and have location. That is why talk about ministry must begin with talk about particular places.

The biblical story is relentlessly particular: Ur, Hebron, Canaan, Jerusalem, Shechem, Samaria, Goshen, Sinai, Jericho, Bethlehem, Nazareth, Capernaum, Galilee, Golgotha, Damascus, Philippi, Fair Havens, Rome. It is impossible to tell the story of Israel and the church, of Jesus and his disciples, without talking about particular places. Most Bibles contain maps, sometimes showing ancient Israel or Jerusalem or perhaps the journeys of Paul. Why? Is it to show, in some graphic form, that this story really happened, that it can in some sense be located? Perhaps. But these maps also suggest that the truth the gospel is seeking to tell us is not a disembodied idea or concept, but a truth that is wrapped up with particular places and their history, with a particular people—Israel and the church—indeed, with a particular person, Jesus Christ. This story, like a family history, cannot be told without rehearsing and remembering where and when and who. And the implication is that to know the truth of this story and to be able to tell it is to be drawn into this family history, to inhabit its body and remember its journey and share in its hope.

Undertaking ministry is to become well acquainted with this family and with the particular places where its life takes shape. That might seem a strange way of thinking about Christian ministry, as if it had something to do with genealogy or geography. Surely, one must begin elsewhere, with biblical study, for example, or pastoral care or even theology. Yet all of these important disciplines are taught for the sake of the body, that is, for the sake of the body's own witness to the joyfully disturbing presence of Christ in the world. And even that is not an intellectual or mental concept. Nor is it a reality that one can embrace without risk. The body of Christ always has an address. Ministry begins with place.

In his book *Open Secrets*, Richard Lischer describes the stomach-churning moment when, having completed seminary, he saw for the first time the church to which he had been called.

When I was a young man, I once saw the cathedral at Chartres shimmering in the morning mist across a field of new-mown hay. It was a revelation, a sudden disclosure of the heavenly world. Like my church, the cathedral lay in an ordinary field on ordinary country roads near ordinary farmhouses, but with its foundation of mist and its towers of stone it was so supernaturally beautiful that it appeared to descend from heaven. . . . My new church did not shimmer in the gloomy November light or appear to descend from any height at all. Instead, its faded red bricks appeared to grow up out of the soil. The twin lanterns beside the entrance were bizarre touches that might have been added by a ship's chandler. In place of a great tower, the building sported a peeling cupola and a steeple with a copper cross from which one arm was mysteriously missing. I could not see anything fine about this church of the one-armed cross. . . . I wasn't so put off by the physical appearance of the church as I was by its obvious irrelevance. My seminarian friends and I reveled in the social and religious ferment of the 1960s. We never tired of posing as progressives and announcing like JFK that we wanted to "make a difference." We had skimmed Augustine's *City of God* but devoured Harvey Cox's best-seller, *The Secular City*. His book reminded us that there was a secular world out there yearning to be liberated from religious superstition, and theological activists like us would be the agent of its redemption. The city was where the action was, not in the suburbs such as the one I grew up in, and certainly not in country churches like this one, with its broken cross and flourishing graveyard. . . . But no, I couldn't even open my car door because that would have been an admission, if only to myself, that this assignment was acceptable. . . . I knew who I was and, with a brand new Ph.D. in Theology already in hand, I had mapped out a distinguished career for myself: a cutting-edge pastoral appointment in a socially conscious but not un-affluent congregation, followed by a professorship in our denominational flagship seminary, capped off by the presidency of the seminary and—why not?—of the whole church body, which to me was the sum of my whole world. . . . Of course, I knew Christendom needed little churches like this one, but I bitterly resented the bureaucrats who had misfiled my gifts, misjudged my obvious promise, and were about to place me in rural confinement. Whoever they were, they hadn't bothered to get to know me. That's the way I felt, and my resentment came quick and fully formed.[10]

Lischer spent three years as pastor of Cana Lutheran Church. He preached to and pastored his flock, baptized and buried and taught and cared for its stolid German farm families. He did not want to be their pastor, and at his installation service, when the bishop's sermon compared the installation of a pastor to a marriage, Lischer thought of it as an arranged marriage, "for this bride and groom had not fallen in love or chosen one another."

The congregation and I were insignificant figures in a larger and older pattern. The church has always identified its potential leaders, indoctrinated them, and then rudely inserted them in some setting or other where they almost never belong. At seminary we brooded over the mysteries of God for four years, only to turn up later as chaplains to covered-dish suppers and car washes with the youth. One part of the church goes to great expense in order to prepare a theologian for another part of the church that wants a guitar player. Like misshelved books, we are *there* waiting to be used, but will anyone ever find us? As partners in an arranged marriage, my congregation and I might fall madly in love, which, in this creaky old church already seemed unlikely to me, or we could accommodate ourselves to what, if we were honest, each of us knew to be a mismatch.[11]

But as he walked down the aisle in the installation procession, Lischer began to notice the Trinity window glimmering with the help of some temporary outdoor lighting put up for the occasion.

Beneath the window the cross of the Victorious Christ was mounted to the wall. The crucified Jesus was robed in royal vestments and giving a two-fingered benediction from the cross. The wooden altar was dressed in red brocade for the fire of the Spirit and the blood of the martyrs. On the nave level of the floor, centered beneath the accumulated symbolism of the Holy Trinity, the crucifix, and the crimson altar, sat my chair, which was actually an easy chair borrowed from someone's parlor, that tonight and only tonight would serve as the seat of honor for the new pastor.

I was moved when I saw the alignment of things. I could only imagine the mysteries of all our lives and how they would unfold beneath the cross and our orthodox window. It didn't concern me that the acolytes had mismatched outfits or that the crucifer was wearing black high-topped sneakers, that the three lights behind the window were a little too specific, that the chair was not a *cathedra*, or that the aisle wasn't all that long or impressive. Because it wasn't an aisle at all anymore but my road to the chair and to my call and my truest self and to the ministry of Christ's church.[12]

Strangely, Lischer found that this road also led straight into the messy and often painful lives of his rural parishioners and, even more surprising, straight to the heart of God. They seemed to occupy the same neighborhood, the triune God and the struggling little church. And the terms of the one seemed to encompass the lives of the other. In the chapter "Our Best Window," he tells the story of a little boy, Darwin, who was being raised by his mother and grandmother. Shortly after his baptism, he toddled off a bulkhead and drowned in his grandmother's pond. The geometry of a stained glass window would seem to be a strange place for describing a mystery that might encompass such unbearable grief.

The Trinity window had come from a St. Louis catalog and was "ecclesiastical boilerplate," diagramming very clearly the classical Trinitarian affirmation of *Deus* at the center of the triangular form and from each point a little canal or highway connecting *Deus* to *Pater* on the left, *Filius* on the right, and *Spiritus Sanctus* at the bottom. Within the space of each of the connecting lines was the word *est*, so that one might read from the center, "God is Father,

God is Son, and God is Holy Spirit." However, between the three points of the triangle were some curvilinear lines that held the words *non est*, so that the diagram could be read as also saying, "the Father is not the Son, the Father is not the Holy Spirit; the Holy Spirit is not the Son, the Holy Spirit is not the Father; the Son is not the Father, the Son is not the Holy Spirit."

To be sure, the diagram was only a diagram and was entirely too pat in presuming to explain God in such geometric terms. But the window seemed to say that God is a community of persons, a community of love, and that we are able to love one another only because at the heart of reality is this triune neighborhood, this courtesy among the persons of God's own life. Lischer writes:

> In Cana, we baptized our babies, celebrated marriages, wept over the dead, and received Holy Communion—all by the light of our best window. We believed there was a correspondence between the God who was diagrammed in that window and our stories of friendship and neighborliness. If we could have fully taken into our community the name *Trinity*, we would have needed no further revelations and no more religion, for the life of God would have become our life.[13]

Perhaps those little "highways," Lischer suggests, are the way God is "grooved" into human relationships. Perhaps this diagram is precisely the kind of thing that keeps us from creating a god after our own image, a god who could prove useful to us. "*Non est*," the window insists on saying. But the Trinity window also says God is for us "and lavishly so," Lischer concludes. The lines make it clear that *Deus est Filius* and *Pater* and *Spiritus Sanctus*.

> Without the God of our best window, we would have found ourselves defenseless in a disordered world, pitting our meager resources of friendship and hope against the charismatic authority of random events, like car wrecks, unwanted pregnancies, heart attacks, anthrax, drought, and death. The window did not explain the senseless things that befell us, but as long as we were convinced that some design underlay the

God we worshiped, it suggested a hidden design in our lives
as well and, like an absurdly delicate barrier, held back the
chaos of the years.[14]

If ministry begins with particular places, with a location, then
perhaps it is because there is a kind of geography within God, a
neighborhood of persons into which we are drawn in Jesus Christ.
To follow him is to be drawn ever more deeply into the neighborhood of the triune God and the life together which the triune
God enacts in Jesus Christ. There is something terribly concrete,
located, particular, and quite unspiritual about Christian ministry.
And that is because the triune God is so located, particular, and
disconcertingly unspiritual in being for us in Jesus Christ, even to
being numbered among the transgressors where he is crucified
not alone, but among a congregation of believing and disbelieving sinners.

Looking out at his congregation on his last Sunday as their pastor, Lischer concludes:

> When I was a boy and later a seminarian, I would have sworn
> that each person makes the race alone, like a long-distance
> runner who has separated from the pack and runs at his own
> pace. Religion was the most refined form of privacy available
> to me. But now, as I looked out upon this cloud of upturned
> faces, each representing others already turned to the light, I
> was embraced by a wholeness I never before experienced. It
> seemed to me that I was looking at the church as God sees it,
> not as a series of individual quirks and opinions, but as a sin-
> gle heart of love and sorrow. The only thing that made us dif-
> ferent from any other kinship group or society was the
> mysterious presence of Jesus in the community. We were his
> body, which is not a metaphor.[15]

That night, Lischer and his family left Cana to take up a new
call in Virginia. The young minister who had not wanted to be
"married" to the congregation in Cana, who wanted instead a
more "significant" charge, looked back over his three years in

ministry there, and confessed: "The poet-preacher John Donne said, 'I date my life from my ministry.' There is more to life than ministry, but I knew as soon as we pulled out of the driveway that I had needed Cana more than Cana ever needed me. I do make sense of my life from that ministry."[16]

Body Language: "The Preaching of the Word of God is the Word of God"

If ministry begins with the place the Word makes, then its primary task is to proclaim that Word and the joyful obedience it makes possible. Preaching is the primary work of the minister. That is why theology's home is really in the parish, because theology has no other reason for being than to aid the church in its mission of proclaiming the gospel. To be sure, ministers must undertake many other activities, from pastoral care to administrative leadership, but their primary work is being servants of the Word, "stewards of God's mysteries" (1 Cor. 4:1).

Ministers are tempted, especially today, not to think of themselves primarily as preachers. And indeed, congregations are tempted to prefer a pastor who is more of a therapist or an administrator (or optimally, a therapist-administrator) than a preacher.[17] Part of this, no doubt, is due to the false understanding abroad in the culture that thinks of the church as a religious nonprofit agency that is about doing good works and offering healing at society's more stressful edges. Managing conflict is its business. Of course, this understanding has a great deal to do with the church's eagerness to accommodate the culture but perhaps even more with the church's own failure to understand itself as the community established by the Word.

One of the reasons the culture is so interested in healing itself or, to put it in more theological terms, in saving itself, is that the church itself has often preached this message. Forgetting its own theology or even belittling it as a hindrance, the church has too often represented itself as a "redemption center" or even a "salvation" or "wholeness" shop, thinking that if it is perceived as such, the culture will somehow be interested in its message. The culture, after all, understands the marketplace, and it is hardly surprising that a church that has jettisoned its theological baggage would be willing to couch its message in terms the market can understand. The joy of the gospel's own message of grace is somehow not enough or too strange, it is thought, to attract significant numbers of adherents; it must be interpreted, explained, or otherwise reduced to something more familiar and marketable. Just so does the faith become about "me" and even encourage "me" to think that I am my own, and that my health, my salvation is the primary reason that churches exist. The culture has no trouble believing this because it is already convinced that "I" am at the center of my own universe. That is the reality in terms of which "I" am taught to think critically, to attract the interest of others, and even to judge what is good or evil, healthy or ill.

In such a culture, preaching the gospel of Jesus Christ will always appear to be a problematic undertaking whose very strangeness may be a sign that its claims are only too well understood. In such a culture, the task of preaching will be pressured to become moralistic (to make a better "me") or therapeutic (to make a happier and healthier "me") or entertaining (to distract "me" from not only other distractions but especially the frightening claims of the gospel itself). Before long, the church that is captive to such a culture will want preaching to cease.

Stephen Webb has argued that modernity has attempted to silence the church's preaching, making us all "a little bit deaf" to the orality of the gospel message. Since obviously God is silent (or transcendently distant), the argument goes, the church must undertake the much quieter and altogether more sensible matter of studying texts critically, of discovering hermeneutical keys or devising theories of inspiration that will help those texts "speak" symbolically.[18] Thus does preaching become explanation, and faith gnosis, and finally, the gospel a form of something else: therapy or entertainment or moral instruction.

How recently the preached word has fallen under suspicion and how different things once looked can be seen in the affirmation of the Second Helvetic Confession (1561): "The preaching of the Word of God is the Word of God." Lest one think this affirmation must die the death of a thousand qualifications, the confession makes it clear that "when this Word of God is now preached in the church by preachers lawfully called, we believe that the very Word of God is proclaimed, and received by the faithful; and that neither any other Word of God is to be invented nor is to be expected from heaven."[19] Moreover, not even the "inward illumination of the Spirit" can eliminate the need for this external act of preaching. The church lives, the confession insists with the Reformers, as it *hears* this Word.

Why did the Reformers think it so important that the gospel be voiced and heard? What is it about the gospel that insists on being vocalized, on being audible? Why is it not enough merely to receive the sacrament, to enjoy the liturgy, or to meditate in silence? All of these are often, in truth, more eloquent than many sermons.

In his *Institutes*, Calvin makes it clear that the "abiding mark" of the true church is that it "hears God's voice."[20] Luther goes so far as to say that the "ears alone are the organs of a Christian man," for justifying faith comes through hearing.[21] The Reformers distrusted the visual not on aesthetic grounds, nor simply because the eye can deal only with surface realities, nor even because beauty itself can all too easily appear cold and distant. Rather, the Reformers believed that God is the *living* God who spoke and speaks and will speak. The God they encountered in Scripture is distinguished from idols precisely in the fact that the God of Abraham, Isaac, and Jacob speaks. God's self-revelation is the Word made flesh. Speaking to us is the way God draws near to us and invites our response. The gods of the idols are silent.

Karl Barth's theology of the Word of God can be read in this sense as an attempt to recover for the church the centrality of God's speech. That was the problem with the liberal theology he inherited (as well as much of Roman Catholic theology), Barth thought: it rendered God silent. Though garrulous, especially about human capacities, liberal theology was largely engaged in a monologue with itself, in which God's voice remained at best a metaphorical way of talking about human religious sensibilities. That way of doing theology, Barth thought, would always be somewhat "hard of hearing" and "unaware of the fact that in relation to God man has constantly to let something be said to him, has constantly to listen to something, which he constantly does not know and which in no circumstances and in no sense can say to himself."[22]

In contrast, the enfleshment of the Word in Jesus Christ means that this Word becomes "hearable."[23] That, for Barth, is the gift of God's self-revelation. In the living Word, God interrupts the silence that threatens to separate us from the love of Christ, allowing this Word made flesh to be heard as a word of life directed to us, a word that invites us to draw near and speak in response to God.

Preaching, then, is quite human speech, in which God "speaks like a king through the mouth of his herald."[24] It is not chatter, nor is it ponderous with self-importance. Rather, it is that joyfully obedient witness, that human witness, that cheerfully unbombastic witness to the God who has overcome the silence and who speaks and has spoken and will speak in Jesus Christ. To the extent that the church acquiesces in the silencing of its own proclamation, the church expresses a death wish, vainly attempting to cut itself off from the source of its own life. "The preaching of the Word of God is the Word of God."

Clearly, there is much bad preaching in the church. Clearly, there is much preaching that has not listened sufficiently to the words or the Word of Scripture. Clearly, the coarsening and cheapening and subverting of words by ideologies, commercial interests, and religion itself make it hard to take any voice seriously amid the clamor of contemporary culture. Yet God speaks. And God's word is truth. None of this is particularly palatable to a culture that would prefer its gods to be silent and would prefer even more that we not talk about the truth. But in fact, only death is silent.[25] The crucifixion can perhaps best be understood as that last, futile effort to render God completely silent, to shut God up in a stone-cold tomb forever. That way, we could talk *about* God as we like and never have to worry about God's speaking *to* us or our speaking *to* God. But the resurrection is the outrageous, embarrassing, even unwanted overcoming of such silence, in the victory of that joyful Word that cannot be contained and insists on being voiced. "Silence," Stephen Webb reminds us, "does not have the last word."[26] The joy of God's victory over death does.

And that joy is articulate. To proclaim this gospel, one must listen intently, but one must also and even more dare to speak.

Humankind's Chief End: The Freedom of the Minister

In his book *After Virtue*, Alasdair MacIntyre argues that modernity has produced certain recognizable characters, who embody its prevailing ethos and perpetuate its moral fictions. These characters are, according to MacIntyre, "the aesthete, the therapist, the manager, and the bureaucratic expert."[27] A common feature of all these types of modernity, MacIntyre argues, is that none of them is particularly interested in ends; they focus their energies on means. They are all concerned with technique, with measurable effectiveness in terms of a particular task or goal. The reason moral discourse is so difficult, if not impossible, with these characters is that none of them are characterized by any professed chief end. Unless one is clear about what human beings are made for, MacIntyre argues, moral discourse becomes impossible, and moral choice finally indistinguishable from "I like this rather than that."

MacIntyre ends his book wondering if what is needed is a new St. Benedict, that is, a new rule for life together in the community. Regardless of what one might think of that possibility, MacIntyre's book masterfully rehearses what happens to a culture that is unable to speak anymore of "man's chief end." And though his purpose is not to speak of ministry per se, his book points implicitly to the danger of the church's ministry being assimilated to one or more of the characters of modern life. It is startlingly easy, in our day, not to talk about ends.

One of the reasons theology matters so in the parish is that it forces ministers to think about ends. "What is man's chief end?" the Westminster Shorter Catechism asks. "Man's chief end is to glorify God and enjoy Him forever." Though the language is archaic and some would say sexist, one ridicules this answer at great peril. Lesslie Newbigin has written eloquently about what happens in a culture that no longer thinks that humanity has this or any particular end. He wonders if "it is possible to believe that concern for minorities, for the poor, for the disabled is important if the fact is that human life is the result of the success of the strong in eliminating the weak."[28] If humanity has no end in the praise of God, then other ends will do. The twentieth century was disastrously full of a number of candidates.

Interestingly, the Shorter Catechism's answer does not say that our chief end is to become saved. Ministry becomes a joy for precisely that reason. Our salvation, strange to relate, is not as important as our culture—and as we ourselves—often think it is. In a culture that is reluctant to talk about humanity's end in God, salvation of self not surprisingly becomes our primary, if often unstated, chief end. We live in a culture that has made an idol of its own salvation, whether religious, political, economic, or cultural. Its particular hell is that it *cannot* forget self. That is why for all its obsession with salvation, its pursuit is finally joyless.

To hear that our chief end in life is to rejoice in what God has done is to hear a countercultural message. It is to be set free from the obsession with our own salvation. Indeed, it is to acknowledge the wonderful gift that in Jesus Christ that matter has been taken care of ("It is through the cross that joy enters the world") and that we are free to live in joy—to forget self, to see our neighbors (and their needs), to rejoice in creation, and to give thanks to God. Osip Mandelstam, Russia's greatest poet of the twentieth century and a Jew, identified this as the source of joy for Christians: because Jesus Christ has redeemed the world, we do not have to pretend that that is our job. We are instead free to "enjoy the world."[29]

The church's ministry has the high calling of delivering this message and reminding the church and the world of this gift, of the glorious freedom that is ours in Jesus Christ to not be anxious about our life (Matt. 6:25) as if our salvation were the point of this story. God's victory in Jesus Christ is the point of this story, and God has made us to rejoice in that victory, to glorify and enjoy God forever, and to summon all of creation to participate in this joy. Worshiping idols is exceedingly boring work, especially idols of our own salvation. Rejoicing in the glory of God, however, never fades or grows tiresome. "His greatness is unsearchable" (Ps. 145:3).

The joy of ministry is quite simply the joy of unfolding this message. There is nothing more intellectually challenging, psychologically demanding, physically exhausting, and theologically satisfying than ministry. It is hard. It is full of disappointments and griefs and even failures. It takes courage. And hope. And often simple, stupid persistence. It is relentlessly embarrassing in the incommensurability of our gifts and the task set before us. Who would want to walk in Jeremiah's shoes or Paul's or even a small-town pastor's for very long? Who would even pretend to "speak the Word of God"?

Yet who would love his own emptiness more than God's abundance? Who would prefer the moral righteousness of his own embarrassment and, like a sulking elder brother, refuse the invitation to the joy of the banquet? Who would miss out on the splendor of standing alongside Jeremiah or Paul or some small-town pastor who must say a very painful, if utterly evangelical, word to a congregation? What if such joy is what we were made for, indeed, what all creation is made for, that is, to participate in the joy of God's own life? To be sure, as Jeremiah or Paul or that small-town pastor might well remind us, the church's ministry cannot be undertaken without groans, but such groaning cannot be given more weight than it deserves. In the end, to enter upon the church's ministry is to know this splendid embarrassment, this joyful passion[30] that is ministry. It is a venture the church risks, confident in the God who is familiar enough with tears to wipe them away from his children, the God who in Jesus Christ puts an end to all mourning and crying and pain. This God's glory "does not allow itself to be diminished" or "to be disturbed in its gladness and its expression of gladness" or even "to be checked in the overflowing of its fullness." The God of Jesus Christ "is eternal joy."[31]

Chapter Seven

Weapons of the Spirit

Finding the Courage to Preach, Teach, and Pastor

If you live today you breathe in nihilism. In or out of the Church, it's the gas you breathe.

—Flannery O'Connor[1]

I think that the Church is the only thing that is going to make the terrible world we are coming to endurable; the only thing that makes the Church endurable is that it is somehow the body of Christ and that on this we are fed. It seems to be a fact that you have to suffer as much from the Church as for it but if you believe in the divinity of Christ, you have to cherish the world at the same time you struggle to endure it.

—Flannery O'Connor[2]

Do you know the Hopkins-Bridges correspondence? Bridges wrote to Hopkins at one point and asked him how he could possibly learn to believe, expecting, I suppose, a metaphysical answer. Hopkins only said, "Give alms."

—Flannery O'Connor[3]

Again this is the best and most useful exercise in humility when he accustoms us to obey his Word, even though it be preached through men like us and sometimes even by those of lower worth than we. If he spoke from heaven, it would not be surprising if his sacred oracles were to be reverently received without delay by the ears and minds of all. For who would not dread the presence of his power? . . . But when a puny man risen from the dust speaks in God's name, at this point we best evidence our piety and obedience toward God if we show ourselves teachable toward his minister, although he excels us in nothing. It was for this reason, then, that he hid the treasure of his heavenly wisdom in weak and earthen vessels (II Cor. 4:7) in order to prove more surely how much we should esteem it.

—John Calvin[4]

Ministry is hard, or perhaps more accurately, ministry is a form of love, the most unsentimentally hard of the Spirit's gifts. It is a commentary on the weakness of our own theology of ministry that we should ever be tempted to think that ministry could be about something else—a strategy, perhaps, or a skill—or that love could ever be thought easy or riskless or even manageable. When Peter was told that Christ's ministry would lead to the cross, Peter rebuked Jesus for even suggesting such a thing, so sure was he that love did not require so dreadful a cost. To be sure, parish ministers are not messiahs, and knowing what Jesus would do in any given situation may not prove all that helpful given the fact that none of us is Jesus. Even our devotional aspiration to "imitate Christ" carries with it more than a little presumption. Still, as Jesus reminds us, there is a cross that is just our size, one that will require all our "energy, intelligence, imagination, and love"[5] to bear.

But to say that ministry is a form of love might lead one to conclude that ministry is about the minister's capacity to be loving or even self-sacrificing, an illusion that ministers themselves sometimes believe and occasionally even propagate. However, that is not what ministry is about either, any more than it is what love is about.

The church exists, the Barmen Declaration reminds us, where "Jesus Christ acts presently as the Lord in Word and Sacrament through the Holy Spirit." As such, the church is always the congregation of "pardoned sinners" bearing witness to Christ's love for this world, and doing so by confessing that it belongs to this One who loves us, and that the church "lives and wants to live solely from his comfort."[6] What makes ministry an act of love is the Yes God speaks to sinners in Jesus Christ. Ministry is, in the first instance, what God does, indeed, the way God loves. God's ministry to the world makes the church's ministry possible. God's Yes in Jesus Christ creates a church of "pardoned sinners" whose ministry it is to dare to speak of the love of God for this world, and to risk the joyful obedience that is the true correspondence to such love made flesh in Jesus Christ. So before ministry is a task, before it is a craft, before it is even a problem, it is God's love active and incarnate in Jesus Christ.

To undertake ministry is to participate in the love of Christ for this world, which is what the church does by preaching, teaching, and offering pastoral care for Jesus' sake. Love is why the Scriptures are carefully exegeted, why the eighth-graders are taken on a mission trip, why Communion is celebrated in the nursing home, why the plight of the poor is a matter of relentless theological concern. It may not look like love, and ministers may not feel particularly loving or regard themselves as examples of the type, but in all these ways and more the love of Christ for this world shapes the church's ministry and its ministers.

But this "love" is not any love. One of the reasons that the Reformers were reluctant to talk about "love of God" as the foundation of ministry was their fear that ministry would soon become a selfish effort to save ourselves by "loving God" with our devotions, prayers, and mystical approaches, leaving our neighbors to fend for themselves. We are called rather, Calvin thought, to trust in God, to have faith in God's faithfulness first of all, "relegating [our] love to a subordinate position"[7] that issues in love of neighbor. But even Calvin admits that love of neighbor is rooted in our love of God, "who bids us extend to all men the love we bear to him, that . . . whatever the character of the man, we must love him because we love God."[8]

The Swiss Roman Catholic theologian Hans Urs von Balthasar thinks that ministry has more to do with love than we might suspect. Indeed, he thinks that faith, at least initially, is less a moral or intellectual response to God than it is an aesthetic one, evoked by a grace that is inherently attractive. "*Charis* refers to the attractive 'charm' of the beautiful, but it also means 'grace.'"[9] To serve this word of grace as a minister is, first of all, "to be lovingly enraptured by the message."[10] One is captured by this story, and indeed, one's imagination is "enraptured" by its beauty. Ministry begins at the point where the "charm" of the story evokes praise, inviting us to enter its delight. We show that we understand this word when we voice its joyous message. Von Balthasar thinks that the response to such proclamation leads ministry into dialogue with the culture, such that the movement is from the contemplative (being "enraptured" by the beauty of the message) to the kerygmatic (proclaiming the goodness of this news) to the dialogical (engaging the culture with its truth).

One does not have to accept the whole of von Balthasar's scheme (though it is deeply provocative) to appreciate the fact that ministry is rightly understood to begin at the point where the gospel's message "charms" us with its vision of love and so captures our hearts that loving this world (and particularly that fractious part of it called church) no longer seems a contemptible chore but the most marvelous gift of all. To be sure, the vision is not just "charming"; we grow in its grace not by admiring the gospel but by a deeper participation in its goodness and truth. Still, it is the gospel's joy that enables us to love ministry, to give ourselves to it, and even more important, to love those with whom we minister.

❧❧❧❧❧❧❧❧❧

If the church's ministry is truly rooted in the love of God revealed in Jesus Christ, then it can be described, at least partially, in terms of the "more excellent way" Paul outlines in his letter to the Corinthian church. Clearly, this "way" makes sense only as it describes the love of Jesus Christ. Because Jesus Christ is who he is, then to be patient or kind or not envious or rude, to be free of resentment or always having to have one's way, to endure things that are unbearable is to be drawn into the "charm" of his loving and to begin to discern the joy of his ministry. Love, faith, and hope are the abiding realities at work here, Paul writes, though he singles out love as the "greatest."

So how does such love inform the work of ministry?

In a 2006 article, William Willimon decries the lack of passion for preaching among recent seminary graduates. He attributes this lack to the rise of the "therapeutic culture" in which preaching has become just another means by which the culture diagnoses and meets its perceived needs. The preacher's task is, accordingly, to be available to the congregation and satisfy its desires. In contrast, he argues that "to be a preacher is to be called to love God more than our congregations."[11] Following Karl Barth, Willimon argues that the best way ministers can love their people is by faithfully preaching the gospel to them.

It is true that ministers are first of all to be understood as "servants of the Word," and that love of God can never be reduced to "keeping the customer satisfied." It is also true that Jesus Christ is head of the church and that love for the church can never supersede our loyalty to him and his Word. But one wonders if what Willimon noticed was not so much the lack of passion for preaching as the lack of love for doing so in the context of the local congregation. If he is right that the most loving service the pastor can render is to preach the Word to a congregation, then if preaching is no longer a passion for seminary graduates, perhaps it is because the congregation is no longer loved or seen as the crucial place which the Word has addressed and called into being. But if that is the case, the problem is not homiletical but theological, or rather, ecclesiological, and the task is not to recover a passion for preaching so much as to find preachers who love congregations passionately enough to preach to them and who believe that preaching the Word gives birth to and nourishes communities of faith.

Willimon is right that serving as a therapist in order to help an affluent culture deal with its problems is a distressingly popular vocational option for seminarians today, but it is so not because preaching seems unattractive but because preaching as an act of love for the mundane, thorny, ridiculous, and all-too-local congregation seems so confining and difficult. But the church's ministry of proclaiming the love of God in Jesus Christ is precisely what creates communities of faith. That is what happens when the gospel is preached, whether in Corinth or Ephesus or Rome or Madras or Shanghai or Kinshasa or Quito or Kansas City. Loving

Jesus Christ first of all, and in any case, enough to proclaim his
gospel causes communities of faith to spring up. That is what the
gospel does. To love Christ is to love Christ's people—which does
not mean to acquiesce in all their desires or to become complicit
in their self-justifying projects. It does mean to embrace the awkward, often selfish, earthen vessel that is the local congregation
and to see it as the place where God hides the treasure of the
gospel. Preaching apart from the life together the Word estab-
lishes makes no sense, and there is no love of Christ that does not
include love of Christ's people.

The two are not the same, however, and to the extent that love
is the "more excellent way," the love that shapes ministry is the
love defined by Jesus Christ. That love both contradicts our other
loves and rightly orders them. If the first priority of ministry is to
love Christ, then following him alone will become the way the
community is most truly built up and his love for the world most
truly rendered visible.

But what does loving Christ mean for the minister? Concretely
it means to be disturbed and charmed and content in his presence;
to love his Word enough to rejoice in its careful study and joyful
proclamation; and to love his body as the weird and at times even
difficult community brought into being by this Word and charged
with the task of showing that it understands this Word by loving
the world. This ministry is rooted in the love of Christ, which
comes to us ever as a gift and which we take up only by participation in him. But it is and ever will be a ministry of love.

In a series of lectures he gave on a tour of America, Karl Barth
ended his reflection on theology and ministry by talking about
love. The love of God, he said, sustains the minister in the work
of ministry, and though it may be sensed only as a "passing thun-
derstorm" that "bursts at one moment here and at another
moment elsewhere," this love is what makes ministry a gift.

> Whether or not the thunderstorm bursts, [the minister] may
> live and work with a *promise*. He is promised that perfect love
> is the heaven spread out over him, whether or not this love
> is momentarily clear or hidden from him. Protected and

encouraged by the promise of this love, he may pray, study, and serve; and trusting in it, he may think, speak, and finally also die. Once a man knows where to seek and from where to expect the perfect love, he will never be frustrated in his attempts to turn himself to it and to receive from it an orientation which enlightens his small portion of knowledge. This love abides. . . . It abides even when theologians come and go and even when things become brighter or darker in theology. It abides like the sun behind the clouds, which more precisely is and remains victoriously *above* the clouds as "the golden sun." . . . It is better to know about this . . . even if all that can be done is to sigh for it. Simply to know about it affords ample occasion to join in the praise of God, the God of the covenant, the God of love itself. It is the very purpose of theological work, at any rate, to know about this love and, therefore, to join in the praise of God.[12]

To be disturbed and charmed and content in the presence of Jesus Christ is to confess that ministry is sustained by his love and is not a religious project we can manage or control. Ministry is not a comfortable vocation. The presence of Jesus Christ has ever been and will always be disturbing. Jesus' disciples were and are often baffled by his word, rarely at ease in his presence, or at least not in such a way that they might presume to be his "buddy" or to have some claim on him. There is very little banter in the New Testament. And worse, Jesus persistently takes his disciples down paths that can only be described as imprudent at best and calamitous at worst. The rich young ruler, for all his timidity and lack of faith, had at least this much in his favor: he saw more clearly than most where this path would lead.

Yet Jesus' disciples chose to follow. The Gospels are remarkably reticent in explaining why this was the case. We read nothing of Jesus' physical characteristics or the nature of his mannerisms or the power of his rhetoric. We read only that he said, "Follow me," and "they left their nets and followed him" (Mark 1:17–18). In the New Testament, Jesus is rarely portrayed as being alone. There are times when he seeks solitude, and other times when his disciples betray and abandon him, but Jesus insists on doing ministry in the company of those whom he has called. Even on the night of his betrayal he chooses to break bread with his own, and when he is abandoned by them, he dies not alone but in the company of sinners. Even Jesus' postresurrection appearances are not descriptions of his personal triumph, much less celebrations of the immortality of his soul, but rather accounts of his bodily presence among the disciples, claiming and reclaiming them for his ministry and mission in the world.

"Charm" may be too clever a way of talking about the Holy Spirit, and indeed, it may be too slippery a word to do justice to the reticence of these Gospel accounts. Still, it is not too much to say that Jesus' disciples, as disturbed and confused as they often appear to be, nevertheless were drawn to him in such a way that they dropped what they were doing and followed him. To be charmed by Jesus is to leave behind some things, indeed, many things that we once thought vital, and to do so quite happily for the sake of being in his presence. It is not a spell he casts but a joy that disturbs and challenges and delights with his presence. At some point, every disciple gives up something that he might have once called "everything" and follows.

But loving Christ not only disturbs or charms, it also gives deep contentment. Contentment is not often considered much of a Christian virtue, especially among those who confuse it with self-satisfaction. We are supposed to be discontent with the way things are, to be "always reformed and always in need of being reformed." And indeed, no one can minister in the name of Jesus Christ for very long without sensing how much of one's own ministry and indeed one's own life needs reforming. We are never to be content with ourselves or with the misery that afflicts so much of our world. Yet the love of Christ that takes the form of ministry to Christ's people brings with it the rarest of gifts in our world: a true sense of contentment. This gift is not to be confused with a sense that one has arrived or, worse, that one will never arrive—both of which tempt the Christian who is on the way—but has to do with the great gift of being called to do something important. Again, that does not mean something prestigious or even impressive, but in the economy of God's love something important.

On his eightieth birthday, Karl Barth reminded his guests of a quotation from Luther that Barth had copied out and addressed to himself when his *Epistle to the Romans* was beginning to make theological waves. Luther cautioned against thinking that because the minister had succeeded in something, he was entitled to consider himself privileged. Feel your ears, Luther advised, and "you will find a lovely pair of big, long donkey's ears."[13] In reflecting on his own ministry, Barth returned to the image of the donkey and reminded the gathered celebrants that a donkey also appears in Scripture.

> It was permitted to carry Jesus to Jerusalem. If I have done anything in this life of mine, I have done it as a relative of the donkey that went its way carrying an important burden. The disciples had said to its owner: "The Lord has need of it." And so it seems to have pleased God to have used me at this time."[14]

Ministry carries an important burden, and though Luther is right that the importance of this burden threatens to make of us self-important asses, Barth is even more right that God has uses for such donkeys, and that being a donkey with this burden brings with it a certain contentment, even a joyful freedom.

Loving Christ means also to love Christ's word. One of the hazards of theological education is the temptation to reduce the preaching task to a matter of critical methodology. The great gift of historical criticism is to slow the preacher down long enough to listen to the text and not just use it to advance a personal agenda. This vitally important task is all too easily belittled in a culture that loves instant messaging. Biblical study and homiletical practice are not simply methods to be employed but are a part of an intellectual adventure in which the life of the mind (as well as the heart and soul) is brought into the church's deep conversation with the gospel's message. That conversation is a feast. Around its table the minister finds church fathers and mothers; intellects of the highest order such as Augustine and Irenaeus, Calvin and Barth; difficult saints such as Simone Weil and Vernon Johns and Maximilian Kolbe; writers such as J. R. R. Tolkien, C. S. Lewis, Flannery O'Connor, and David James Duncan; poets such as Dante, Shakespeare, Donne, Herbert, Hopkins, Auden. Who would not want to enter into that conversation? Who would not find such a feast a delight when trying to find the words to proclaim Christ's Word? Much has been made of ministry's arduous administrative and therapeutic and even exegetical labors. Why is the intellectual adventure of preaching, of studying Scripture, of straining to engage the culture with the power of this Word, even of listening to the way the culture has been engaged at other times and places by this Word, why is this not the passion of a lifetime? Who else gets to do this *each week*? Why does our study of Scripture and the joy of its proclamation not make us dance as joyfully as the Torah does for Jews who have completed the cycle of its readings? Why does the love of Christ's Word not describe for us exactly the joy of ministry?

In 1934, when Karl Barth was forced to leave Germany, he spoke a final word to his students from the University of Bonn: "So listen to my last piece of advice: exegesis, exegesis and yet more exegesis! Keep to the Word, to the scripture that has been given us."[15] Barth was not recommending exegesis for the sake of greater proficiency in the historical-critical method but precisely so that as these students entered the unimaginable darkness that was about to descend on them, they might "keep to the Word" that would be their light and would sustain the church in its witness to the light, which not even that darkness could overcome. There was no weapon of the imagination or of faith that could engage the principalities and powers at sufficient depth except the Word of God. Exegesis, the sustained discipline of participating in the church's listening and conversation with Scripture and preparing to proclaim it, introduces us to the same intensity of passion in the work of ministry today.

And the same joy. "What a book the Bible is," says Father Zossima in a last sermon to his fellow priests.

It is like a mold cast of the world and man and human nature. Everything is there, and a law for everything for all the ages. And what mysteries are solved and revealed: God raises Job again, gives him wealth again. Many years pass by and he has other children and loves them. But how could he love those new ones when the first children are no more, when he has lost them? Remembering them, how could he be fully happy with those new ones, however dear the new ones might be? But he could, he could. It's the great mystery of human life that grief passes gradually into quiet tender joy. . . . I bless the rising sun each day, and as before, my heart sings to meet it. But now I love even more its setting, its long slanting rays and the soft tender gentle memories that come with them, the dear images from the whole of my long happy life—and over all the Divine Truth, softening, reconciling, forgiving! My life is ending. I know that well. But every day that is left me I feel how my earthly life is in touch with a new infinite, unknown, but approaching life, the nearness of which sets my soul quivering with rapture, my mind glowing and my heart weeping with joy.[16]

❖❖❖❖❖❖❖

Though love is the "greatest of these," according to Paul, faith and hope also abide, and they offer the minister weapons of the Spirit as well. In bringing this chapter to a close, a brief consideration of what those might be is in order.

If the joy of ministry grows out of Christ's love for the world, then Christ's faithfulness is what shapes that ministry into a grateful heart. Grace and gratitude, faith and ministry always go together. That may be obvious, yet it is surprising how subversive a weapon the gift of gratitude is, and how powerful.

It is common to speak of some seminary students today as "second-career" students. But ministry is not really a career, even for "first-career" students. A career does not beggar one quite like ministry. A career is possible, even achievable, even perhaps successful. Ministry calls one to speak the Word of God to folk.

114 *The Joy of Ministry*

Where are the credentials that make that possible? Ministry calls one to proclaim, "I am the resurrection and the life," as a family is standing around an open grave. How successful is that? Ministry calls one to enter the darkness of other lives and even confront the darkness within one's own life armed with nothing more than the rumor of Christ's victory. That is no romantic quest but a journey where one fails and falls again and again, often looking ridiculous, able only to sigh for what one is unable to see.

Yet one sighs. If ministry were only a career, such sighing would be worse than useless, but in response to the promise of God's grace, this sighing is a form of gratitude, a way that our tiredness enters into the praise of God. In her essay "The Love of God and Affliction," Simone Weil writes, "When an apprentice gets hurt or complains of fatigue, workmen and peasants have this fine expression: 'It's the trade getting into his body.'"[17] So do even the sighs of ministry bear witness to the grace that has gotten into our bodies and evoked such gratitude and praise. And so do even our sighs become weapons of the Spirit, reminding us that this journey is not about our careers at all, but the grace of our Lord Jesus Christ who has called us to this impossible work and given us the gift of sharing in his sighing and his joy. One need not count one's blessings to know that ministry can be done only with a grateful heart. Anything less would be only a career. That is the great weapon of the Spirit that is given to those who confess that they belong not to themselves but to their faithful Savior, Jesus Christ.[18]

Two other weapons are crucial for ministry. Both faith and hope share equally in them. The first might be called "stupid persistence" or, perhaps more charitably, perseverance, endurance, or faithfulness. But stupid persistence has much to recommend it as a Christian virtue and as a part of the minister's arsenal.

Good ministry does not happen fast. In the book of Acts, Luke seems fond of quantifying the Spirit's work, drawing attention to the increasing number of believers in the early days of the church. But most growth is slow, and some of the most important growth is very slow. In truth, ministry most nearly resembles farmwork, in that much the same tasks have to be performed each week. A sermon's shelf life is extraordinarily brief; it must be replaced almost as soon as it is preached. Pastoral calling, teaching, and administration all relentlessly demand the minister's time and come with their own urgencies and crises. Yet all these tasks probably could be performed without that stupid persistence that is so essential to the minister.

This gift comes when the darkness descends, when the way ahead is not clear, when it is painful to love, when life together seems more of a burden or even a torture than a gift. Then one stupidly persists in ministry. One keeps walking in the dark and does the next thing to be done. It is ridiculous to pretend that such moments do not occur in ministry or even that they do not occur very often. They do, and far too often. But faith and hope work most of the time not by lifting us up to a high mountain but by giving us strength to keep on when we cannot see the way forward, even to be stupidly persistent, trusting that we are in the company of One who knew what it was to "set his face toward Jerusalem" and keep walking. There is even a kind of joy that comes from such stupid persistence, a joy that ministers often recognize in each other, acknowledging the miracle of doing ministry when nothing can be done except to wait, to endure, to live with not knowing, and to do the next thing. That is a gift, a weapon of the Spirit with which both faith and hope are well acquainted.

Finally, there is prayer. This weapon might be thought to be a pious way to bring this chapter on ministry to a close. But prayer in ministry is where all the blood is, where the sighs are sighed, where the hurts are voiced, where the psalms of lament as well as the psalms of praise are sung. Ministry is not possible without prayer. And the reason is that at its heart, prayer is petition; it is asking for help. Yes, it is also gratitude, also praise, also intercession, but all these things are impossible even to express without the help of the Holy Spirit who teaches and enjoins us to ask. Ministry, at its heart, is about asking. That is why it is so difficult. One need not "ask" to succeed in a career. But then a career is always possible. Ministry, on the other hand, is a gift. It comes to us not because we ask for it, but it does not come without the asking. Indeed, faithful ministry makes those who participate in it even more bold in their asking. Our culture finds asking humiliating and often thinks that strength means never having to ask. That is why prayer is so difficult for us and why ministry is so easily assimilated to our notions of career, a move that renders ministry hopeless. But in truth, asking, daily asking for God's help, praying "thy kingdom come," is the surest way that a minister participates in Christ's transformation of the world. It is a sign of hope. It is a sign that the minister understands both from whence cometh his help and whose ministry this is. It is also a sign that the minister is now prepared to do the really hard work that the gift of ministry involves, engaging "the principalities and powers" not with his own paltry self-sufficiency but with the gifts of that "bounteous God"[19] whose bounty is more ready to give than we are to ask.

John Calvin's description of prayer as "the chief exercise of faith" is remarkably unsentimental. He compares prayer to a shovel, by which "we dig up . . . the treasures that were pointed out by the Lord's gospel, and which our faith has gazed upon."[20] Prayer is a form of digging, and ministry involves daily, unglamorous, thoughtful spadework. That is how faith hopes: by digging. Prayer is the shovel.

❧❧❧❧❧❧❧❧

Many other practices or virtues sustain ministers in their calling. Some are mentioned in Scripture; others are not. A good minister must love to read, must love learning, must understand the public nature of the gospel and even the political nature of the kingdom. A good minister will cultivate the company of others—other pastors, colleagues, friends—with whom to share the work and joy and burdens of ministry. No one can minister alone for very long, and it is not a good model of ministry to speak of "solo pastors." Ministry as practiced in most Protestant churches today is far too lonely a business already, which is one reason its joy has been obscured. The gift of ministry is a shared thing, even a conversation into which one enters.

None of these weapons of the Spirit, as important as they are, can sustain ministry by themselves, even with assiduous practice. Ministry belongs to Jesus Christ, the living Lord, and it is in his name and in his company that one dares to minister.

In the last year of his life, Karl Barth was interviewed on the radio about Mozart and theology. Some of the conversation centered on the meaning of the word "grace." Before requesting a last piece to be played (Mozart's *Missa Brevis* in D Major), Barth had this to say about his own ministry:

> Grace is also only a provisional word. The last word, which I have to say as a theologian and a politician, is not a concept like "grace" but is a name: Jesus Christ. *He* is grace, and *he* is the last, beyond the world and the church and even theology. We are not able to "control" him. But we have to do with him. What I have attempted during my long life has been in increasing measure to lift up this name and to say: *"There ...!* There is no salvation except in this name. For grace, is also there. There also is the impulse to work, to struggle, the impulse for community, for human fellowship. Everything, which I have tested in my life, in weakness and in foolishness, is there. *But there it is."*[21]

There, in Jesus Christ, is the joy of ministry. There, in him, in the risen Lord! All our self-centered heroics and clever methodological strategies are buried in a tomb. But he is not there. He refuses to be silent or sad. He has gone before us and beckons us even now to come and follow, and to rejoice in his company and in his ministry.

Chapter Eight

Minimum Salary

A Commencement Meditation*

Text: John 16:16–33

One of the best commentaries on the Gospel of John is Dostoyevsky's *The Brothers Karamazov*, a novel which also has a good deal to say about theological education. I want to begin by quoting at length a passage from that novel that has to do with a novice priest who has recently graduated from a theological school of sorts and who is struggling to discern the particular shape of God's call upon his life. What precipitates the crisis that animates this scene is the discovery on the student's part that his mentor, his beloved professor and teacher, is not a saint. Perhaps for most students at Union-PSCE such a discovery comes well before graduation, but for Alyosha—that is this student's name—for Alyosha the discovery that his mentor, Father Zossima, is not only mortal but is subject to the same humiliation that death brings to us all, that discovery almost shatters his faith. He knew that his teacher would die, but he had thought that his teacher's saintliness would have preserved the old man from the corruption of death and render him a kind of relic, bearing mute witness to his own holiness. But that is not what happened. Like Lazarus, the dead Father Zossima soon "stinketh." Upon discovering this and in confusion and

---

*This sermon was a commencement meditation for Union Theological Seminary and Presbyterian School of Christian Education, Richmond, May 28, 2005.

119

despair, Alyosha flees the monastery, wanders about the town, and returns, exhausted, late at night only to find another monk sitting beside the coffin of his beloved teacher, reading the Gospel text aloud.

Alyosha sits down in the darkened room and tries to pray. His prayers, however, are interrupted by the monk's reading of the Gospel lesson. So, reluctantly, he begins to listen. The monk is reading from John 2, the story of the wedding at Cana. "And when they wanted wine, the mother of Jesus saith unto him, 'They have no wine.'" "Ah yes," Alyosha thinks to himself, "I was missing that, and I didn't want to miss it, I love that passage: it's Cana of Galilee, the first miracle. . . . Ah, that sweet miracle! It was not men's grief, but their joy Christ visited. He worked his first miracle to help men's gladness . . . 'He who loves men loves their gladness.' . . . 'There's no living without joy.'"[1] As Alyosha continues to listen, he dozes off, and in a dream his former teacher comes to him in a vision, his tired old face now crinkled in a smile. "We are rejoicing," the little, thin old man tells him. "We are drinking the new wine, the wine of new, great gladness. Do you see how many guests are tasting the new wine? . . . Do you see our Son, do you see Him?"

"I dare not look," whispers Alyosha.

"Do not fear him. He is terrible in his greatness, awful in his sublimity, but infinitely merciful. He has made himself like unto us from love and rejoices with us. He is changing the water into wine that the gladness of the guests may not be cut short."[2]

Alyosha wakes from the dream, looks again at the coffin to reassure himself that his former teacher is actually dead, and then makes a decision. He turns sharply away, going down the steps and out of the monastery entirely. He leaves his school behind and does not look back.

> He did not stop on the steps either, but went quickly down; his soul, overflowing with rapture, yearned for freedom, space, openness. The vault of heaven, full of soft, shining stars, stretched vast and fathomless above him. The Milky Way ran in two pale streams from the zenith to the horizon. The fresh, motionless, still night enfolded the earth. The

white towers and golden domes of the church gleamed out against the sapphire sky. . . . The silence of earth seemed to melt into the silence of the heavens. The mystery of earth was one with the mystery of the stars. . . .
Alyosha stood, gazed out before him and then suddenly threw himself down on the earth. He did not know why he embraced it. He could not have told why he longed so irresistibly to kiss it, to kiss it. But he kissed it weeping and watering it with his tears, and vowed passionately to love it, to love it forever and ever. "Water the earth with the tears of your joy and love those tears." His elder's words echoed in his soul. . . .
Within three days, he left the monastery in accordance with the words of his teacher, who had bidden him to "go forth into the world."[3]

Well, that's enough for now; you have been patient to listen to such a long stretch of a long novel, though I do not apologize for reading it to you upon the occasion of your graduation. Indeed, if we had time, I would read more and would, in any case, encourage you, if you have not already done so, to read this novel, which has so much to say about the human heart and the joy that sustains those who undertake the risk of teaching and preaching the Gospel of Jesus Christ. But, in truth, it is the joy Alyosha comes to know that I want you to see, and to see it not as a virtue or as a kind of optimistic spirit to be cultivated or even the musings of a "beautiful soul," but as "the minimum salary," the gift that is paid regularly, if surprisingly and sometimes quite subversively, to those who offer themselves in Christ's service. "Water the earth with the tears of your joy," Alyosha, the seminary graduate, remembers his teacher telling him; it is not men's grief but their joy Christ visited.

So what do you make of this scene of passionate joy? A mystic caught in an ecstatic moment who is both enraptured and perhaps also disturbed? A student momentarily paralyzed at the prospect of leaving the friendly confines of a seminary campus for the more daunting world outside? And kissing the earth and watering it with tears of joy? When was the last time such an over-the-top liturgical act made sense to decent and orderly Calvinists?

I think that if we are honest with ourselves, we are a bit embarrassed with Alyosha's antics and don't know quite what to do with such joy. Yet strangely Scripture embarrasses us in much the same way. "Then our mouth was filled with laughter," the psalmist writes, "and our tongue with shouts of joy" [Ps. 126:2]. "Who for the sake of the joy that was set before him endured the cross," the author of Hebrews [12:2] reminds us in a phrase that stands in stark contrast to more recent depictions of the passion. Love may be the first fruit of the Spirit, but the second is joy [Gal. 5:22], which Paul has no trouble turning into a verb, enjoining us to "Rejoice in the Lord always; again I will say, Rejoice" [Phil. 4:4]. In the Synoptics, the complaint most often voiced against Jesus is not that he is grimly prophetic, but rather that he is a "glutton and a drunkard" who enjoys the life of the party a bit too much, and inevitably with the wrong people [Matt. 11:19]. In John's Gospel, as we have heard read this morning, Jesus talks to his disciples about that joy a new mother knows, a joy that includes labor pains that may well be full of tears but which are soon put aside when the child is laid in her arms. That joy, he says to his disciples, is the property that rightfully belongs to those who follow Jesus Christ. "So you have pain now; but I will see you again, and your hearts will rejoice, and no one will take your joy from you" [John 16:22].

I suspect that for many of us "joy" seems a harmless thing, an ornament, perhaps, to the Christian life but not its essence. It is easy for us to assimilate the word to our notions of optimism or fun or positive thinking or even being in a good mood, all pleasant and even marketable commodities but sustainable only if one ignores the harsher realities of disease, poverty, oppression, and death. *Candide*, one suspects, is modernity's take on joy: a naive pleasure indulged in only by fools, by people who do not really know what is going on. "Those who are laughing," Brecht once said, "have not heard the terrible news." After all, how can one be joyful in the face of so much suffering? Life is a serious business. You may be forgiven even today for thinking that the past three years or so have been devoted to the serious business of learning to exegete a biblical text or engage in the exhausting tasks of pastoral care or undertake the demanding work of preparing to teach, all for the sake of taking seriously a world that is very serious about itself and its own needs. Alexander Schmemann, in noting the almost obsessive seriousness of our own culture, especially the seriousness of its games and entertainments, asks, "How can one be joyful when so many people suffer? How can one indulge in festivals and celebrations when people expect from us 'serious' answers to their problems?"[4] He then goes on to describe how the church often forfeits its claim to joy precisely at this point, and always in the name of some good work or serious cause. "Christians have accepted the whole ethos of our joyless and business-minded culture. They believe that the only way to be taken 'seriously' by the 'serious'— that is, by modern man—is to be serious, and therefore, to reduce to a symbolic minimum what in the past was so tremendously central in the life of the church—the joy of a feast."[5]

We work so hard to do without joy, even to the point of specifying what is the absolute minimum we can believe and still retain the good opinion of the all-too-serious modern world. But "the absolute minimum," while entirely respectable, is not enough; it is not enough to sustain you in ministry or to sustain a life in faith. "It was not men's grief, but their joy Christ visited," Alyosha discovers. The gospel is large, unmanageable, embarrassingly beautiful, extravagant enough to make you embrace the earth and even kneel to kiss it, enough to send you out of a seminary, not trying to preserve all you have learned for fear of losing it, but crazy enough, foolish enough, joyful enough to spend it all on a world— or what is harder, on a congregation—in any case on folk who are busy reconciling themselves to the sad wisdom of death and do not quite know what to do with a gospel of resurrection joy.

It is that sad wisdom I would warn you of today. That is the wisdom that seeks to preserve its life and even justify itself, and it is the wisdom, I regret to tell you, that pervades our churches and pulpits and is not unknown even in our life together as a seminary. Such sad wisdom is what Alyosha thought would be vindicated if his sainted teacher had been preserved in death as a relic, and such sad wisdom is what is overcome in the joy of the feast that Alyosha hears in the story of the wedding at Cana. That is the joy that converts him from being reconciled to death and its very "spiritual" ways, to embracing the earth in all its delicious earthliness. That is why joy is so unornamental and why it has so little to do with the immortality of the soul and so much to do with the resurrection of the body.

The work upon which you are about to embark is so much not a career, so much not even a second career, but more like a fearsome quest or pilgrimage, full of dragons, a long obedience that will engage you with principalities and powers quite beyond your imagining. Our culture's image of a pastor or a teacher does not envision anything so dangerous or so demanding. Pastors and teachers are thought to be helpers who are nice people who do kind things for others and are unobjectionable if harmless folk. This is an image, I believe, by which our culture attempts to reassure itself that it is well insulated from the severe mercies of God's grace. Yet, I tell you that as pastors and teachers you will see the power of death divide races in the communities to which you are called, divide churches which you will pastor, and even tear apart nations and families and marriages. This power of death is able to divide a pastor's own heart and lead him or her to the very depths of despair. And precisely here, you will be asked to help. You will be asked, daily, to enable folk to live with less than what the gospel promises, to get by with a "symbolic minimum" of the gospel's story. You will be asked not to preach or teach anything as radical or extravagant or as beautiful as resurrection hope, but rather to offer explanations, even to explain death, to help folk become adjusted to that final reality. Such help is not an unpleasant task. A culture bent on pursuing its own happiness has a way of rewarding those in the helping professions and is always eager for the gospel to prove itself useful in one way or another. But precisely here, you must learn to say no. Precisely here you must learn to laugh and to rejoice in the gospel's glorious lack of explanation, lack of resignation, lack of seriousness, and celebrate instead the divine comedy that insists on embarrassing us with its feast of bread and wine, of resurrection joy, of its crude, subversive, even outlandish insistence that Jesus lives. That news does not help the world further its agenda, especially not its sad agenda of resignation to death and the deadly ways we justify ourselves or make our theologies more acceptable to the pursuit of its happiness. Yet as Master Calvin would remind us, the gospel is not first of all about our own salvation. Indeed, I hardly need to tell you that our only real comfort is that we belong, body and soul, in life and in death, *not to ourselves* but to One who is faithful and who is relentlessly ingenious if not downright sneaky in drawing us out of our agendas into his life, making us "wholeheartedly willing and ready from now on to live for him."[6]

How sneaky this One is can be seen in the fact that the gospel you are called to serve is not merely good or true, or even powerful, but is, as Alyosha discovered, surpassingly beautiful. That may be what we least expect of the gospel, that it is . . . beautiful. But that is why joy is so much at the center of the faith, why the Christian life is, among other things, an aesthetic response, a way of living "gracefully" before the God of grace, the way of learning to dance before the God whose life as Father, Son, and Holy Spirit the church fathers thought best described in terms of a dance. Do not hurry to make this grace a thing of moral rectitude. We Calvinists have much to answer for in that regard. But first of all, rejoice. As the text says, though you will soon "be scattered, each one to his own home," be of good cheer. Living gracefully is the gift of that One who has overcome the world.

Let me end with two more quotes from Dostoyevsky. The first is from a sermon given by Father Zossima describing to graduating seminarians the "minimum salary" of faith. He says:

> My friends, pray to God for gladness. Be glad as children, as the birds of heaven. And let not the sin of men confound you in your doings. Fear not that it will wear away your work and hinder its being accomplished. Do not say: "Sin is mighty, wickedness is mighty, evil environment is wearing us away and hindering our good works from being done." Fly from that dejection![7]

But how is one to do such a thing, to keep disappointment and even despair over one's own efforts at bay? How are we to "rejoice always," to "be glad," and what would it look like if such a miracle were to occur?

At the end of the novel, Alyosha has found himself among a group of boys, one of whom has died after a long illness. The boy who died, whose name is Illusha, had been an outsider, the butt of jokes and object of ridicule, until Alyosha came and brought a measure of reconciliation and peace. There are twelve boys who are following Alyosha, and this clear reference to the New Testament is made unmistakably clearer when Alyosha talks to his twelve disciples on the way to the funeral breakfast. Kolya, the leader of the boys, asks Alyosha, "Karamazov, can it be true as they teach us in church, that we shall all rise again, all, Illusha, too?" And Alyosha replies with the beautiful, simple, but wholly mysterious truth of the gospel: "Certainly we shall all rise again, certainly we shall see each other and shall tell each other with joy and gladness all that has happened." Alyosha says this, half laughing. "Oh how wonderful it will be!" cries Kolya. "Well, now," Aloysha says, "we will finish talking and go to his funeral dinner. Don't be disturbed at our eating pancakes—it's a very old custom and there's something nice in that! Well, let us go! And now we go hand in hand."[8]

How does joy overtake us amid all our seriousness and lethal efforts to become reconciled to the sad wisdom of death? As it did the two disciples on the road to Emmaus, or those who were fishing all night with nothing to show for it, or those huddled in an upper room locked against the world, it creeps in when we weren't looking for it, and surprises us with the presence of the risen Lord, who will surprise you in your teaching and pastoring and studying. "A little while, and you will no longer see me, and again a little while, and you will see me" [John 16:16]. So even though there is pain and longing and disappointment and defeat, "I will see you again, and your hearts will rejoice, and no one will take your joy from you."

It is the risen Lord, alone, who saves us from the hopeless pursuit of happiness and makes our work instead so full of joy. Well, now, let us go. And now we go hand in hand. Amen.

Notes

Chapter 1: A Cluster of Grapes

1. Ephraim Radner, *The End of the Church* (Grand Rapids: Wm. B. Eerdmans Publishing Co., 1998), 354.
2. Eugene Peterson, *Under the Unpredictable Plant: An Exploration in Vocational Holiness* (Grand Rapids: Wm. B. Eerdmans Publishing Co., 1992), 16.
3. David B. Hart, "Lengthened Shadows, VII," *New Criterion* 22 (March 2004): 5–18.
4. Alexander Schmemann, *The Journals of Father Alexander Schmemann, 1973–1983*, trans. Juliana Schmemann (Crestwood, NY: St. Vladimir's Seminary Press, 2000), 137.
5. Alexander Schmemann, *For the Life of the World: Sacraments and Orthodoxy* (Crestwood, NY: St. Vladimir's Seminary Press, 1998), 53.
6. Ibid., 53.
7. This reference is to Neil Postman's book *Amusing Ourselves to Death* (New York: Penguin Books, 1986). See also Timothy K. Beal's *Roadside Religion* (Boston: Beacon Press, 2005), and his discovery in Kentucky of a "Golgotha Fun Park."
8. Schmemann, *For the Life of the World*, 55.
9. See the last line of George Herbert's poem "Love (III)" in *Everyman's Poetry* (London: J. M. Dent, 1996), 89.
10. Søren Kierkegaard, *Philosophical Fragments*, trans. David F. Swenson, translation revised by Howard V. Hong (Princeton, NJ: Princeton University Press, 1969).
11. Schmemann, *Journals*, 193.
12. Simone Weil, *Waiting for God*, trans. Emma Craufurd (New York: Harper & Row, 1973).
13. See C. S. Lewis's autobiographical account of his pilgrimage in the faith, *Surprised by Joy* (New York: Harcourt Brace Jovanovich, 1984). The title is a play on his wife's name but clearly also an attempt to identify what for Lewis was the heart of the gospel.
14. As reported by Richard John Neuhaus in *First Things*, November 2003, 13.
15. Schmemann, *Journals*, 117.

16. Ibid., 82.
17. Schmemann, *For the Life of the World*, 90.
18. David James Duncan, *The Brothers K* (New York: Bantam Books, 1996), 613.
19. Fyodor Dostoyevsky, *The Brothers Karamazov*, trans. Constance Garnett (New York: Sinet, 1980), 699.
20. Karl Barth, "The Holy Day," in *Church Dogmatics*, III/4, The Doctrine of Creation, ed. G. W. Bromiley and T. F. Torrance (Edinburgh: T. & T. Clark, 1969), 47–72. (Hereafter cited as *CD*.)
21. Ibid., 68.
22. Ibid., 69.
23. A good introduction to Herbert's poetry can be found in *The Temple: The Poetry of George Herbert*, Christian Classics, ed. Henry L. Carrigan (Brewster, MA: Paraclete Press, 2001). Though I have not followed him entirely, I have been helped by David Daniell's interpretation of this poem in *The Bible in English* (New Haven, CT: Yale University Press, 2003), 466–69.

Chapter 2: Dostoyevsky as an Apostle of Joy

1. William Tyndale, *Prologue to Luther's 1522 New Testament*, as cited in David Daniell, *William Tyndale: A Biography* (New Haven, CT: Yale University Press, 1994), 123.
2. Barth, *CD* III/4:376.
3. Peterson. *Under the Unpredictable Plant*, 49.
4. Ibid., 59.
5. Joseph Frank, *Dostoyevsky: The Mantle of the Prophet, 1871–1881* (Princeton, NJ: Princeton University Press, 2002), 570.
6. Charles Taylor, *Sources of the Self: The Making of Modern Identity* (Cambridge, MA: Harvard University Press, 1989), 452.
7. Dostoyevsky, *Brothers Karamazov*, 297.
8. Ibid., 59.
9. Ibid., 37.
10. Ibid., 52.
11. Ibid.
12. Ibid., 53.
13. W. H. Auden, "For the Time Being" (chorus 3), in *Collected Poems*, ed. Edward Mendelson (New York: Vintage International, 1991), 353.
14. Simone Weil, "Evil," in *The Simone Weil Reader*, ed. George Panichas (New York: David McKay, 1977), 382.
15. *The Habit of Being: Letters of Flannery O'Connor*, ed. Sally Fitzgerald (New York: Vintage Books, 1979), 129.
16. Dostoyevsky, *Brothers Karamazov*, 54.
17. Ibid.
18. Ibid.
19. Ibid., 54–55.

20. Ibid., 55.
21. Ibid., 56.
22. Ibid., 56–57.
23. Ibid., 57.
24. Ibid., 56.
25. Most famously, Alyosha, after leaving the monastery. Ibid., 334.
26. Taylor, *Sources of the Self*, 451.
27. See the parable Alyosha tells Grushenka in the chapter titled "An Onion."
28. Dostoyevsky, *Brothers Karamazov*, 222.
29. Ibid., 223.
30. Ibid., 226.
31. David B. Hart, "Tsunami and Theodicy," *First Things*, no. 151 (March 2005): 6–9.
32. Taylor, *Sources of the Self*, 451.
33. Dostoyevsky, *Brothers Karamzov*, 227.
34. Ibid., 243.
35. The term is Charles Taylor's. He notes that the Russian word for "schismatics" is *raskolniki*, a tipoff that Ivan and Raskolnikov (in *Crime and Punishment*) are close kin (*Sources of the Self*, 451).
36. Dostoyevsky, *Brothers Karamazov*, 700.

Chapter 3: Laughing through the Tears

1. Karl Barth, *Dogmatics in Outline*, trans. G. T. Thompson (New York: Harper & Row, 1959), 123.
2. Karl Barth, *Ethics*, ed. D. Braun, trans. Geoffrey Bromiley (New York: Seabury Press, 1981), 507.
3. Eberhard Busch, Jürgen Fangmeier, and Max Geiger, eds., *Parrhesia*: Fröhliche Zuversicht: Karl Barth zum 80. Geburtstag am 10. Mai 1966 (Zurich: EVZ Verlag, 1966).
4. Eberhard Busch, *Karl Barth: His Life from Letters and Autobiographical Texts*, trans. John Bowden (Philadelphia: Fortress Press, 1976).
5. Eberhard Jüngel in *Karl Barth, 1886–1968. Gedenkfeier im Basler Münster* (Zurich: EVZ Verlag, 1969), 47–50 (my translation).
6. Bruce McCormack, for example, in *Karl Barth's Critically Realistic Dialectical Theology: Its Genesis and Development, 1909–1936* (Oxford: Oxford University Press, 1997), has little or nothing to say about joy as a theological category in the development of Barth's theology or the delight in knowing God that Barth thought he learned from Anselm. Similarly, William Stacy Johnson's book on Barth (*The Mystery of God: Karl Barth and the Postmodern Foundations of Theology* [Louisville, KY: Westminster John Knox Press, 1997]) treats Barth as if his most interesting attribute was his theological virtuosity, an obvious point that ignores Barth's passionate joy in putting his genius in service to the church. Academic efforts to "explain" Barth in terms of his interpretive moves

invariably miss the one thing that needs to be noted above all: the happy and confident witness his theology makes to the God who graciously elects to be our God and elects us to be God's people. Barth's theology is *Church Dogmatics* and is undertaken for the sake of the church and its mission. Two more recent interpretations of Barth that do not fail in this regard are Eberhard Busch, *The Great Passion*, trans. G. W. Bromiley, ed. Darrell L. Gruder and Judith J. Gruder (Grand Rapids: Wm. B. Eerdmans Publishing Co., 2004), and Joseph Mangina, *Karl Barth: Theologian of Christian Witness* (Louisville, KY: Westminster John Knox Press, 2004).

7. Hans Urs von Balthasar, *The Theology of Karl Barth*, trans. Edward T. Oakes, SJ (San Franciso: Ignatius Press, 1992), 25–26.
8. Dietrich Bonhoeffer, *Letters and Papers from Prison*, ed. Eberhard Bethge (New York: Macmillan, 1971), 229.
9. Mangina, *Karl Barth*, 177.
10. Ibid., 177–78.
11. Karl Barth, *Evangelical Theology: An Introduction*, trans. Grover Foley (New York: Holt, Rinehart & Winston, 1963), 12.
12. Karl Barth, *Church Dogmatics*, I/1 (Edinburgh: T. & T. Clark, 1975), 61–62.
13. Barth, *Evangelical Theology*, 164.
14. Barth, *CD* I/1:87.
15. Ibid., 52.
16. See F. D. E. Schleiermacher, *The Christian Faith*, ed. H. R. Mackintosh and J. S. Stewart (Edinburgh: T. & T. Clark, 1968), 194: "All attributes which we ascribe to God are to be taken as denoting not something special in God, but only something in the manner in which the feeling of absolute dependence is to be related to Him."
17. See Mangina, *Karl Barth*, 31.
18. Karl Barth, *The Word of God and the Word of Man*, trans. Douglas Horton (London: Hodder & Stoughton, 1928), 186.
19. See Martin Rumscheidt, *Revelation and Theology: An Analysis of the Barth-Harnack Correspondence* (Cambridge: Cambridge University Press, 1972), especially 7–19.
20. Barth, *CD* III/3:298.
21. Karl Barth, *Wolfgang Amadeus Mozart*, trans. Clarence K. Pott (Grand Rapids: Wm. B. Eerdmans Publishing Co., 1986), 55.
22. Barth, *CD* III/3:298.
23. Barth, *Wolfgang Amadeus Mozart*, 53.
24. Barth, *CD* II/1:647.
25. Ibid., 655.
26. Ibid., 659.
27. Ibid., 661.
28. Ibid.
29. Ibid., 663.

30. Ibid., 664.
31. Ibid., 665.
32. Ibid.
33. Ibid., 676.
34. See Augustine, *On Christian Doctrine*, in *Nicene and Post-Nicene Fathers of the Christian Church*, vol. 2, ed. Philip Schaff (Grand Rapids: Wm. B. Eerdmans Publishing Co., 1983), 523.
35. Barth, *CD* II/1:656.

Chapter 4: Joy Obscured

1. Flannery O'Connor, *Mystery and Manners*, ed. Sally and Robert Fitzgerald (New York: Noonday Press, 1969), 161–62.
2. In *Christian Century*, May 16, 2006, the editorial "Novel Faiths" notes the gnostic aspects of Dan Brown's novel *The Da Vinci Code* and the Left Behind series by Tim LaHaye and Jerry Jenkins. For a more scholarly treatment of Gnosticism, see Hans Jonas, *The Gnostic Religion* (Boston: Beacon Press, 1958).
3. Dostoyevsky, *Brothers Karamazov*, 297.
4. This brief taxonomy is taken from Philip Lee, *Against the Protestant Gnostics* (New York: Oxford University Press, 1987), chap. 2, "Gnosticism as a Heresy," 13–44.
5. Robert Bellah, *Habits of the Heart* (Berkeley: University of California Press, 1985), 221.
6. Robert D. Putnam, *Bowling Alone: The Collapse and Revival of American Community* (New York: Simon and Schuster, 2000).
7. Harold Bloom, *The American Religion* (New York: Simon and Schuster, 1992). "Obsession with the vagaries of Orphism and Gnosticism, of Enthusiasm and Antinomianism, seems to be the driving principle of my concern with what I call the American Religion. . . . The new irony of American history is that we fight now to make the world safe for Gnosticism, our sense of religion" (30).
8. See Irenaeus, *Adversus Haereses*, a selection and translation of which appears in *Early Christian Fathers*, ed. Cyril C. Richardson (Philadelphia: Westminster Press, 1953), 343–97.
9. Dostoyevsky, *Brothers Karamazov*, 295–96.
10. Charles Taylor does not use this term but describes its content in *Sources of the Self*, 452.
11. Ibid.
12. Dostoyevsky, *Brothers Karamazov*, 307.
13. Ibid., 310.
14. Ibid., 314.
15. Ibid., 320.
16. Ibid., 323.
17. Ibid., 324.
18. Ibid., 329.

19. Ibid, 332–33.
20. Ibid., 333–34.
21. David Johnson, "Making Theology Come Alive in the Parish," *Pro Ecclesia* 3, no. 4 (Fall 1994): 401.
22. Ibid., 402.

Chapter 5: Practicing the Scales of Rejoicing

1. As quoted in Arthur Kirsch, *Auden and Christianity* (New Haven, CT: Yale University Press, 2005), 21.
2. Clarence Brown, introduction to *Hope Against Hope*, by Nadezhada Mandelstam, trans. Max Hayward (New York: Modern Library, 1999), xxii.
3. Arthur C. McGill, *Death and Life: An American Theology* (Philadelphia: Fortress Press, 1987), 70. Just as McGill thought the loss of worship marked a secular society, so the hell of a secular age is characterized by its boredom.
4. Flannery O'Connor, "Revelation," in *Flannery O'Connor: The Complete Stories* (New York: Farrar, Straus & Giroux, 1987), 508.
5. Ibid., 509. The best commentary on this scene is found in Ralph Wood, *The Comedy of Redemption* (Notre Dame, IN: University of Notre Dame Press, 1988), 130–132.
6. The reference is to the last verse of Charles Wesley's hymn "Love Divine, All Loves Excelling." See also the translation of *The Divine Comedy* by John Ciardi (New York: New American Library, 1970), 16 and 872. When Dante at last sees Beatrice in paradise, she looks down on him and smiles, but then as the symbol of divine grace, she turns back to the Eternal Fountain, bearing witness to the source of life and truth and joy.
7. Barth, *CD* III/4:53.
8. Ibid.
9. See Charles Peguy's wonderful poem "Sleep," in *Basic Verities*, trans. Anne and Julian Green (New York: Pantheon Books, 1948), 209–15. "I don't like the man who doesn't sleep, says God." See also W. H. Auden's essay *"Hic et Ille,"* in which he invites existential theologians to preach a sermon on "The Sleep of Christ" and adds, "One of the most horrible, yet most important, discoveries of our age has been that, if you really wish to destroy a person and turn him into an automaton, the surest method is not physical torture, in the strict sense, but simply to keep him awake, i.e., in an existential relation to life without intermission." *The Dyer's Hand* (New York: Vintage International, 1988), 103.
10. Barth, *CD* III/4:56.
11. See Ernest Becker, *The Denial of Death* (New York: Free Press, 1997).
12. Barth, *CD* III/4:68.
13. As cited in Kirsch, *Auden and Christianity*, 58.
14. As cited in Robert McAfee Brown, introduction to *Portrait of Karl Barth*, by George Casalis, trans. and ed. Robert McAfee Brown (New York: Anchor Books, 1964), xiii. The quote is taken from an article by Johannes A. Lombard

in *Antwort*, a Festschrift for Barth on his seventieth birthday (Zollikon-Zurich: Evangelischer Verlag, 1956), 895.

15. Barth, *CD* III/4:77.
16. Ibid., 68.
17. Ibid., 69.
18. Ibid.
19. Ibid., 71.
20. This I take to be the burden of Stephen Webb's argument in his provocative book *The Divine Voice* (Grand Rapids: Brazos Press, 2004).
21. Barth, *CD* III/4:90.
22. Ibid., 75.
23. Ibid., 78.
24. Ibid., 107.
25. The phrase comes from Auden's poem "For the Time Being." "The happy morning is over, / The night of agony is still to come; the time is noon; / When the Spirit must practice his scales of rejoicing."
26. Barth, *CD* III/4:371.
27. Karl Barth, *How I Changed My Mind* (Richmond: John Knox Press, 1966), 86.
28. Barth, *CD* III/4:375.
29. Ibid., 375–76.
30. Hesketh Pearson, *The Smith of Smiths: Being the Life, Wit, and Humor of Sydney Smith* (Pleasantville, NY: Akadine Press, 1999), 230. The life and writings of Sydney Smith are worth studying if for no other reason than for the joy to which they bear such eloquent witness.
31. Barth, *CD* III/4:376.
32. Ibid., 378.
33. Ibid., 378–79.
34. Ibid., 380.
35. Eberhard Bethge, *Dietrich Bonhoeffer*, rev. and ed. Victoria J. Barnett (Minneapolis: Fortress Press, 2000), 150 and 427. See also, Bonhoeffer, *Letters and Papers from Prison*, 304. Bonhoeffer was the most ungnostic of twentieth-century theologians. His confidence in the gospel's power to embody its claims in a concrete time and place regularly caused him to speak unapologetically of the joy, as much as the cost, of discipleship.
36. Barth, *CD* III/4:383.
37. Ibid., 384.
38. W. H. Auden, "The Globe," in *The Dyer's Hand*, 177.

Chapter 6: The Splendid Embarrassment

1. Barth, "The Task of Ministry," in *The Word of God and the Word of Man*, 216.
2. Dietrich Bonhoeffer, *Life Together*, trans. John Doberstein (London: SCM Press, 1956), 9–10.
3. Pearson, *Smith of Smiths*, 224.

4. Charles Williams, *The Forgiveness of Sins* (Grand Rapids: Wm. B. Eerdmans Publishing Co., 1942), 22–23.

5. Ibid., 24–26.

6. Peterson, *Under the Unpredictable Plant*, 22.

7. Ibid., 24.

8. William Willimon, "The Spiritual Formation of the Pastor: Call and Community," in *The Pastor's Guide to Personal Spiritual Formation* (Kansas City: Beacon Hill Press of Kansas City, 2005), 25.

9. The phrase is originally from Paul (1 Cor. 6:19) but is powerfully voiced by John Calvin in his description of the Christian life. "We are not our own: let not our reason nor our will, therefore, sway our plans and deeds. We are not our own: let us therefore not set it as our goal to seek what is expedient for us according to the flesh. We are not our own: in so far as we can, let us therefore forget ourselves and all that is ours. Conversely, we are God's." John Calvin, *Institutes of the Christian Religion*, 3.7.1; ed. John T. McNeill, trans. Ford Lewis Battles (Philadelphia: Westminster Press, 1967), 690.

10. Richard Lischer, *Open Secrets* (New York: Doubleday, 2001), 10–11.

11. Ibid., 48–49.

12. Ibid., 46–47.

13. Ibid., 81.

14. Ibid., 83.

15. Ibid., 232.

16. Ibid., 238.

17. See William Willimon, "Pastors Who Won't Be Preachers: A Polemic against Homiletical Accommodation to the Culture of Contentment," *Journal For Preachers* 29, no. 4 (Pentecost 2006), 37–42.

18. Webb, *Divine Voice*, 165–67.

19. *The Constitution of the Presbyterian Church (U.S.A.)*, Part I, *Book of Confessions* (Louisville, KY: Office of the General Assembly, Presbyterian Church (U.S.A.), 2002), 5.004.

20. Calvin, *Institutes* 4.2.4.

21. As cited in Webb, *Divine Voice*, 144.

22. Barth, *CD* I/1:61.

23. Ibid., I/2:167. Stephen Webb draws out the implications of this statement for the task of preaching in *Divine Voice* (177).

24. Barth, *CD* I/1:52.

25. Ibid., 141: "But death is dumb."

26. Webb, *Divine Voice*, 179.

27. Alasdair MacIntyre, *After Virtue* (Notre Dame, IN: University of Notre Dame Press, 1984), 73.

28. Lesslie Newbigin, *The Gospel in a Pluralist Society* (Grand Rapids: Wm. B. Eerdmans Publishing Co., 1989), 17.

29. Brown, introduction to *Hope Against Hope*, xxii.

30. See Eberhard Busch's introduction to the theology of Karl Barth, *The Great Passion*. I have been helped throughout by Busch's insights.
31. Karl Barth, *Church Dogmatics*, II/1, ed. G. W. Bromiley and T. F. Torrance (Edinburgh: T. & T. Clark, 1964), 648.

Chapter 7: Weapons of the Spirit

1. O'Connor, *The Habit of Being*, 97.
2. Ibid., 90.
3. Ibid., 164.
4. Calvin, *Institutes* 4.3.1.
5. The Constitution of the Presbyterian Church (U.S.A.), Part II, *Book of Order* (Louisville, KY: Office of the General Assembly, 2005–07; G-14.0405, question 8).
6. *Book of Confessions*, 8.17.
7. Calvin, *Institutes* 2.8.53.
8. Ibid., 55.
9. Hans Urs von Balthasar, *The Glory of the Lord: A Theological Aesthetics*, vol. 1, *Seeing the Form*, trans. Erasmo Leiva-Merikakis, ed. Joseph Fessio, SJ, and John Riches (San Francisco: Ignatius Press, 1982), 34.
10. Edward T. Oakes, "Hans Urs von Balthasar (1905–88): The Wave and the Sea," in *Theology Today* 62, no. 3 (October 2005): 367.
11. Willimon, "Pastors Who Won't Be Preachers," 37.
12. Barth, *Evangelical Theology*, 205–6.
13. Karl Barth, "Speech on the Occasion of His Eightieth Birthday," in *Fragments Grave and Gay*, ed. Martin Rumscheidt, trans. Eric Mosbacher (London: Collins, 1971), 113.
14. Ibid., 116.
15. As quoted in Busch, *Karl Barth*, 259.
16. Dostoyevsky, *Brothers Karamazov*, 267.
17. Simone Weil, "The Love of God and Affliction," in *The Simone Weil Reader*, 449–50.
18. See question 1 of the Heidelberg Catechism, *Book of Confessions*, 4.001.
19. O may this bounteous God
    Through all our life be near us,
    With ever joyful hearts
    And blessed peace to cheer us;
    And keep us in God's grace,
    And guide us when perplexed,
    And free us from all ills
    In this world and the next.

    Martin Rinkart, "Now Thank We All Our God," in *The Presbyterian Hymnal* (Louisville, KY: Westminster John Know Press, 1990), 555.

20. Calvin, *Institutes* 3.20.2.
21. Karl Barth, "Musik für einen Gast," in *Letzte Zeugnisse* (Zurich: EVZ-Verlag, 1970), 30–31; my translation.

Chapter 8: Minimum Salary

1. Dostoyevsky, *Brothers Karamazov*, 331.
2. Ibid., 333.
3. Ibid., 333–34.
4. Schmemann, *For the Life of the World*, 53.
5. Ibid., 55.
6. Heidelberg Catechism, *Book of Confessions*, 4.001.
7. Dostoyevsky, *Brothers Karamazov*, 295.
8. Ibid., 700.